W9-CIF-303

General Editor: M. Rolf Olsen

TAVISTOCK LIBRARY OF SOCIAL WORK PRACTICE

Women, the Family,
and Social Work

LIBRARY
College of St. Francis
JOLIET, ILLINOIS

Women, the Family, and Social Work

EDITED BY

EVE BROOK AND ANN DAVIS

TAVISTOCK PUBLICATIONS
London and New York

First published in 1985 by
Tavistock Publications Ltd
11 New Fetter Lane, London EC4P 4EE

Published in the USA by
Tavistock Publications
in association with Methuen, Inc.
733 Third Avenue, New York, NY 10017

© 1985 Eve Brook, Ann Davis
General editor's foreword © 1985 M. Rolf Olsen

Photoset by Rowland Phototypesetting Ltd
Bury St Edmunds, Suffolk
and printed in Great Britain by
Richard Clay (The Chaucer Press) Ltd
Bungay, Suffolk

All rights reserved. No part of this book may be
reprinted or reproduced or utilized in any form
or by any electronic, mechanical or other
means, now known or hereafter invented, including photocopying and recording, or in any
information storage or retrieval system, without
permission in writing from the publishers.

British Library Cataloguing in Publication Data
Women, the family and social work. – (Tavistock
library of social work practice)
1. Social service
I. Brook, Eve   II. Davis, Ann, *1948–*
316.3   HV40

ISBN 0-422-77940-7
ISBN 0-422-77950-4 Pbk

Library of Congress Cataloging in Publication Data
Women, the family, and social work.
(Tavistock library of social work practice)
Bibliography: p.
Includes indexes.
1. Social work with women – Great Britain – Addresses,
essays, lectures.   2. Family social work – Great Britain – Addresses,
essays, lectures.   3. Feminism – Great Britain
– Addresses, essays, lectures.
I. Brook, Eve.   II. Davis, Ann.   III. Series.
HV1448.G7W66 1985   362.8'3'0941   84-26769

ISBN 0-422-77940-7
ISBN 0-422-77950-4 (pbk.)

362.83
B869

Contents

123,545

PART III Towards feminist practice

General editor's foreword

In recent years the feminist analysis of social problems has proved to be a stimulating factor on established academic disciplines. It has also challenged assumptions and revealed a host of social problems that used to have 'no name', and has shaken taken-for-granted assumptions. So far, however, the movement has made little impact on the theory and practice of social work, an area in which personal encounters are numerically dominated by women clients and workers. Given this dominance of women on both sides of social work encounters, and their position within the family and society, this needs to be rectified.

This book remedies this situation by examining the relationship between women, the family, and social work from a feminist perspective. In so doing it provides an exciting reappraisal of the theory and practice of social work and of our understanding of the major problems presented by clients to social work agencies. It has a great deal to offer to workers and their departments in understanding the problems faced by their clients, and in working towards solutions for the 1980s.

This volume has been written by teachers and practitioners primarily for practitioners and students of social work and the personal social services, but also for those who work in the allied fields of health, education, and other public services. It is one of a series designed to represent the collaborative effort of social work academics, practitioners, and managers. In addition to considering the theoretical and philosophical debate surrounding the topics under consideration, the texts are firmly rooted in practice issues and the problems associated with the organization of the services. Therefore the series will be of particular value to undergraduate and postgraduate students of social work and social administration.

The Tavistock Library of Social Work Practice series was prompted by the growth and increasing importance of the social services in our society. Until recently there has been a general approbation of social work, reflected in a benedictory increase in manpower and resources, which has led to an unprecedented expansion of the personal social services, a proliferation of the statutory duties placed upon them, and major reorganization. The result has been the emergence of a profession faced with the immense responsibility of promoting individual and social betterment, and bearing a primary responsibility to advocate on behalf of individuals and groups who do not always fulfil or respect normal social expectations of behaviour. In spite of the growth in services these tasks are often carried out with inadequate resources, an uncertain knowledge base, and as yet unresolved difficulties associated with the reorganization of the personal social services in 1970. In recent years these difficulties have been compounded by a level of criticism unprecedented since the Poor Law. The anti-social work critique has fostered some improbable alliances between groups of social administrators, sociologists, doctors, and the media, united in their belief that social work has failed in its general obligation to 'provide services to the people', and in its particular duty to socialize the delinquent, restrain parents who abuse their children, prevent old people from dying alone, and provide a satisfactory level of community care for the sick, the chronically handicapped, and the mentally disabled.

These developments highlight three major issues that deserve particular attention. First, is the need to construct a methodology for analysing social and personal situations and prescribing action; second, is the necessity to apply techniques that measure the performance of the individual worker and the profession as a whole in meeting stated objectives; third, and outstanding, is the requirement to develop a knowledge base against which the needs of clients are understood and decisions about their care are taken. Overall, the volumes in this series make explicit and clarify these issues; contribute to the search for the distinctive knowledge base of social work; increase our understanding of the aetiology and care of personal, familial, and social problems; describe and explore new techniques and practice skills; aim to raise our commitment towards low status groups which suffer public, political, and professional neglect; and to promote the enactment of comprehensive and socially just policies. Above all, these volumes aim to promote an understanding which interprets the needs of individuals, groups, and communities in terms of the synthesis between inner needs and the social realities that impinge upon them, and which aspires to develop informed and skilled practice.

M. Rolf Olsen, 1985

List of contributors

Eve Brook is a welfare rights worker in Birmingham. She has taught sociology to social workers at Birmingham University and has been active in Women's Aid and youth work with girls.

Ann Davis is a lecturer in Social Work and Social Policy at Birmingham University. She has worked in local authority residential social work and field social work. She is currently involved in welfare rights work and 'Women working with Women' in Birmingham. Previous publications include *The Residential Solution* (1981) London: Tavistock.

Mary Langan is a senior lecturer in Applied Social Studies at Sheffield City Polytechnic. She has worked as a local authority social worker and senior social worker in Wiltshire and the London Borough of Tower Hamlets. Publications include 'The Public Face of Feminism' (in *Making Histories* (1982) London: Hutchinson) and editorship of *The Interventionist State 1880–1920* (forthcoming) Hutchinson.

Jane Calvert teaches sociology at Birmingham Polytechnic where she organizes the certificate course in working with women and girls. She is the joint convener of the British Sociological Association Sexual Divisions Group and was a founder member of the Birmingham Rape Crisis Centre.

Sue Llewelyn is a clinical psychologist at the Department of Psychology, Nottingham University. She was born in Nairobi and educated in the United Kingdom. She specializes in individual and group psychotherapy and is engaged in research into therapeutic factors.

Glenys Parry is a research fellow in Clinical Psychology at the Department of Psychiatry, University of Southampton. She is researching the effects of paid employment and other factors on depression in working class women with young children. She is a member of the MRC/SSRC Unit's psychotherapy research team and editor of *Changes* (the psychology and psychotherapy journal).

Dulcie Groves is a lecturer in Social Administration at the University of Lancaster and a graduate of the Bryn Mawr College School of Social Work (USA). Her current research interests are in the field of income maintenance and relate especially to issues regarding women and social policy. She is working on a study of women and occupational pensions.

Janet Finch is a lecturer in Social Administration at the University of Lancaster. She has researched and published on the sociology of the family and sexual divisions. Her current research and teaching include aspects of social policy affecting women. She is active in the British Sociological Association and its Women's Council, having been on the Association's national executive since 1980.

Janet Finch and Dulcie Groves have co-authored several publications on the topic of women and community care, including an edited book *A Labour of Love: Women, Work and Caring* (1983) London: Routledge and Kegan Paul.

The Birmingham Women and Social Work Group (81) included women working as probation officers, local authority social workers, and residential social workers. The women contributing to a chapter in this book were: Cynthia Bower, Sally Cherry, Teresa Davies, Ann Gilbert, Linda Hartley, Amanda Lamb, Jenny Parrott, Christine Rogers, Pam Trevithick, Bernadette Wilkinson, and Sarah Williams.

Introduction

Books of social work readings come in many forms. Some have a unity of theory; some are unified by their subject matter; and some share the same political concerns. While the latter two are true of this book, the goal of a unified theoretical approach has not been part of our task. Each chapter of this book considers, from a feminist viewpoint, one aspect of the relationship between women, the family, and social work. Together they do not promote a single feminist theory. This is not just because as yet there is no single widely accepted and developed feminist theory of the family and social work. It is also a reflection of the nature of feminism today. The Women's Movement in Britain has emerged as a decentralized, non-hierarchical force that has emphasized the importance of personal experience in developing theory and practice. As a consequence, it embraces a diversity of theoretical approaches. It is this creative and challenging diversity that we aim to reflect in this book. To impose a formal, theoretical unity on our contributors would have been to deny the continuously evolving and questioning nature of feminism.

However, as each chapter demonstrates, there are some common principles that are held by us all. Chief among these is the proposition that we see the roots of women's oppression not only in the general problems of a capitalist society, but also in the very nature and implications of gender. In other words, we live in a world that is not only capitalist but also *patriarchal*. Much of what is discussed in this book stems from this premise. Our understanding of the nature of social work is that as a 'caring profession' it is not immune from the power games of patriarchy, and the consequences of this need to be analysed, understood, and confronted.

It is indisputable that social work at the present time faces considerable problems. There is confusion between the arguments over what social work *is* and what it *should* be, and much of its practice is questioned. Social work appears to have lost its nerve and does not know in which direction to go. Social workers who are very committed to their jobs are getting depressed over heavier caseloads, constant new responsibilities, their lack of 'success', and most important, the difficulties that emerge from each new government cut in public expenditure.

These problems are to some extent internal, but external attacks on social work have deepened and intensified. Academics and politicians ask whether social work 'works' and they argue about value for money. What social workers appear to offer is often presented as the 'soft option', or 'too radical', and certainly 'non-cost effective', in that it cannot be proved that the client is 'better adjusted' or 'less of a problem' after the social work intervention. Consequently, it is often argued that social workers should adopt a more limited and 'scientific' approach, a medical model with 'proper' notions of cause and effect (as if people were no more complicated than bacteria). This means an approach that 'gets to grips' with personal pathology such as child abuse, delinquency, and senile dementia and that does not concern itself with social and political issues over which it has no control.

As feminists we are perturbed by attempts within social work training to take this path and to ignore the complex interrelationships between personality, the family, and the wider social world. Indeed, even in the area where social work theorists feel safest – the personal – we consider that there is in fact a very inadequate understanding of subjectivity, relationships, love, sexuality, egotism, and our inner lives. Too much still rests on 'common sense' assumptions about what constitutes masculinity and feminity, and there is no attempt to consider the manner in which these ideas are socially constructed. In fact, many contributors to social work theory have worked hard to separate a consideration of the individual from such forces as production, reproduction, ideology, and the state. In doing this they follow another 'common sense' view of the world: that personal life (particularly in the family) and the outside world are unconnected. This view has gained impetus since World War I, as family reforms have been largely divorced from concern with the productive process. Real needs of family life have been ignored (for instance the effect on family life of constant shift work) in favour of legislating for an 'ideal' family unit.

In this book we look at the central premise of feminist theory – that the personal is the political – and look at social work in the light of this insight in an attempt to find a form of social work practice that does not dehumanize the client by perceiving her as a unit in the production of surplus value, nor as a victim of incorrect socialization. We are interested in what feminism can offer to the current debate about social work theory and practice by exploring both the subjective and political dimensions of the relationship that exists between women, the family, and social work.

In the first part of this book we concern ourselves with some of the historical and theoretical aspects of this relationship. We examine the development of social work as an occupation, and the consequences of this development for women as workers and clients. We then turn to one of the current theoretical approaches in social work – the unitary approach – to see what it can offer to an analysis of women, the family, and social work. In the second part we concentrate on client groups. The groups we have selected are those that dominate the caseloads of statutory social workers in Britain. They are women who are mothers, women with mental health problems, and women who are elderly. We look at each of these groups in terms of the insights provided by a feminist analysis. We look at the fresh perspectives such an analysis throws on the experiences of motherhood, mental distress, and old age and their implications for social workers. In the final part of the book we look at the consequences that this kind of analysis has for social work practice. We learn of the experiences of a group of women social workers who are grappling with the problems of developing a feminist social work practice against the often hostile reactions of male colleagues and the state agencies who employ them.

We are very aware of how narrow an area of social work we have covered in this book. We have not addressed ourselves to the work taking place in the many voluntary and private organizations that contribute to welfare provision. We have not considered the distinct problems faced by women clients and workers who are not white. We have not dealt with the difficulties faced by disabled women. These areas, and many more, need to be subjected to a feminist social work analysis.

Finally, we would like to thank our contributors who, while demonstrating that there are no easy answers, emphasize the importance of changing the question.

We would also like to thank our typists Sue Gilbert, Irene Hardy, Linda Murphy, and Bobby Spice for their patience in deciphering our scrawl.

PART I ————————————

Women as social workers

1
Women and social work

ANN DAVIS AND EVE BROOK

Introduction

Most of the workers at the front line of the personal social services
in Britain are women. As receptionists, home-helps, volunteers,
residential workers, social work assistants, and field social workers,
they find themselves rationing and 'personalizing' the services offered
by statutory and voluntary welfare organizations (CSO 1981).

At the same time, most of the individuals who come into contact
with these workers are women, for women outnumber men in the
elderly and the physically and mentally disabled populations (Goldberg 1979; HMSO 1982). Furthermore, women (as relatives and
friends) are the main source of 'community care' for these groups
(EOC 1979; Wilkins 1979). The child care services are predominantly
involved with women as mothers, foster mothers, and child-minders.
Even work with probation clients, who are mainly men, involves
extensive contact with women who are wives and mothers, relatives
or friends (Walker and Beaumont 1981).

On both sides, therefore, women dominate the social work encounter. In this chapter we want to look at how this state of affairs
developed. To do this we wish to examine three themes. First, the
growth of social work as a woman's occupation and its assumed
congruence with feminine qualities. Second, the main changes that
have occurred in women's lives and the popular conception of the
family from the nineteenth century to the present day. Third, the
broader social policy and welfare issues that have affected the lot of
women as recipients and providers of welfare in Britain.

4 Women, the Family, and Social Work

Where state welfare services intervene in the personal and social problems that individuals and families experience, it is mainly with and through women as its agents, ministering to other women. This highlights the position women have in the family and in the occupational structure of British society – positions which are *reinforced* by welfare provision. Viewed as the linchpin of family life, women are held responsible by welfare agencies, not just for their own behaviour and attitudes, but also for the behaviour and attitudes of their children, husbands, and relatives. Their position in the occupational structure means that whatever their formal qualifications, they are more likely to find themselves working directly with people and servicing others, than men. They are also less likely to find themselves in powerful decision-making positions such as management, Parliament, and local authorities (Ashworth 1979; EOC 1982). Therefore, decisions about the development of welfare and the resources given to it are usually made by men. The statistics available on staffing in the personal social services (see *Table 1*) show clearly that as one moves away from the front line of welfare one leaves behind the territory of women and enters the territory of men.

Table 1   The staffing of social service departments

position	male	female	male %	female %
Director of social services	95	9	91	9
Deputy director	77	13	86	14
Divisional/assistant director	345	78	82	18
Area director/manager	420	175	71	29
Team leader	2558	1369	54	46
Senior social worker	574	818	41	59
Social worker	3897	6835	36	64
Social work assistant	445	2177	17	83

Source: DHSS personal social services local authority statistics. Certain key staff year ending 1976 England (three authorities omitted to return figures).

In this book we are exploring the position of women in relation to one small area of the personal social services – social work. We are looking at the way in which women as workers and clients become involved in this area, and ways in which they experience it. We also hope to shed new light on the most familiar problems they will encounter.

This is not a topic that has attracted a great deal of attention in social work literature over the last thirty years. Its neglect is interesting, given that the changes that have taken place in the scope and organization of social work during this period have resulted in an increasing number of women being drawn into its sphere. The significance and consequences of the predominance of women in the day-to-day negotiations between social workers, clients, and their families have not been explicitly discussed. Most social work literature has taken for granted that this is a normal, and therefore unimportant, fact of professional life. As such, it has never been given the kind of consideration that has rested on such issues as effectiveness, professionalization, and the bureaucratization of social work.

The impetus for focusing on this topic has come from outside the mainstream of social work literature. It is the result of the activities and thinking of the feminist movement over the last decade. Women in this movement have been concerned with analysing and changing the position of women, and to this end it is they who have highlighted the crucial relationship that exists between women and the family. They have focused, too, on the part which the Welfare State plays in shaping and determining that relationship (Land 1978; Land 1979). The relationship between women, the family, and the state is one of overwhelming significance for all who seek social change.

This growing volume of work has raised difficult and interesting questions for social workers, but there appears to have been some reluctance in both the traditional and radical camps within the profession to take these ideas further. While radicals look for an alternative social work practice, they often ignore feminist research, writing, and action, which have generated a wealth of ideas that are relevant to developing theory and practice in social work. This apparent lack of interest in feminist ideas contrasts sharply with the way in which they have been considered in other areas of welfare, for example, in health care (Leeson and Gray 1978; Roberts 1981).

Elizabeth Wilson's work stands alone, in that from the inside she has asserted that, 'an analysis of the position of women is not marginal but central to a true understanding of the nature of the welfare state' (Wilson 1977:39), and she has begun to explore the influence of social work on women's consciousness *and* the potential contribution of feminist ideas to the theory and practice of social work (Mayo 1977; Wilson 1977; Bailey and Brake 1980). It is from Wilson's assertion that we begin to look at the position of women on both sides of the encounters that are part of social work.

The roots of social work

In reading the accounts of the way in which social work has developed from its nineteenth-century roots to the present day, one becomes aware of two things. First, that until 1945 the experiences of women as workers in the field of social work did merit some explicit discussion. This theme then drops from the post-war agenda. No matter what the organization: the voluntary sector, the probation service, the health service, or local government service, a focus on the lot of women as workers disappears from the late 1940s onwards. It is as if the growth of the personal social services rendered negligible the distinct experiences of women and men employees (Parry and Parry 1979).

Second, where the specific experiences of women in the pre-war period are discussed, a particular group of women dominate the discussion: women from the middle and upper classes. There is little written about the experiences of women in the lower ranks of welfare work and residential care. There are, not surprisingly, even fewer voices from the clients' side. In consequence, the picture we are presented with is a very partial one.

Like all British history, the history of social work is the history of an élite. Women with leisure and money have given much to the development of social work and it would be churlish to deny their contribution. However, the casual ignoring of lower-grade workers and clients in their biographies and other accounts is frustrating for anyone trying to see how and why the profession developed the way it did. Not that these privileged women were free from oppression. They were denied leadership of the occupation that they were creating in response to the needs that they were identifying. Once a structure had become established, their path was not upwards towards management, but sideways into training. Then, as now, decisions were taken by men and largely implemented by women (Walton 1975).

The emergence in the nineteenth century of voluntary and statutory welfare provisions in a developing capitalist economy, raised questions about the proper place of middle- and upper-class women.

The separation of home and work (the public and private domains) that occurred with industrialization had meant for this group of women a retreat from the outside world of work and public life, and entry into the realm of domesticity. It was taken as a measure of the economic success of husbands and fathers if they could afford to keep their wives and daughters in idleness (Oakley 1974). Of course, with at least a quarter of adult women unable to marry and make this world their own, owing to an insufficiency of men, there were a lot of intelligent women with time on their hands and an urge to make themselves useful in some genteel, Christian, and respectable occupation.

The new economic order generated new social problems. Partly through working-class agitation, partly through fear of revolt, partly for philanthropic reasons, and partly to maintain the health of the work force, the state increased its intervention into the domestic world of working-class families. Social workers began to play a key role in this form of intervention and it was from the ranks of middle- and upper-class women that the first social workers were drawn (Walton 1975; Hollis 1979).

There were two major sources of recruitment to this new occupation. The first were the much publicized group of women who, from the 1840s, had been surplus to the requirements of the male population. For this group of unmarried women philanthropy offered an occupation. In these 'pioneering' days the salary was not important (many were unpaid). The gain, they were informed, had to be measured in terms of fulfilment. As a group denied matrimony, good works, though not an absolute substitute, were a good second best. Mary Carpenter's message in an article in the *Women's Journal* in 1858 on 'Women's Work in the Reformatory Movement' was typical of many.

> 'We call, then, on Christian women, who are not bound by their pecuniary circumstances to work for their own living . . . to some earnest work for the good of others . . . and those who are mothers in heart, though not by God's gift on earth, will be able to bestow their maternal love of those who are more to be pitied than orphans made so by the Lord.'   (Carpenter in Hollis 1979:236)

The second source of labour were those married women whose energies were not fully used in the management of their own homes and families. For this group good works were seen as offering a natural outlet, in that it allegedly called on nothing more than those domestic skills that they had successfully developed as wives and mothers.

Louisa Twining in her campaign to attract such women into the area of Poor Law work argued in 1885 that:

'Poor Law work is specifically fitted for women; it is only domestic economy on a larger scale. Accustomed to regulate her own house, a lady has had the management of children and looked after their health, their clothing and education; she has ordered in household supplies and is accustomed to examine into their prices and quality, and finally, she knows something of the requirements of the sick room. Enlarge a household and it becomes a workhouse; multiply the servants by tens and the children by hundreds and you have a workhouse school; increase the sick room and it becomes an infirmary, so that every woman who has managed her own household with wisdom and economy possesses the qualities chiefly necessary in a guardian of the poor.'   (Hollis 1979:249)

These domestic skills were also seen as those which needed to be taught to the 'inadequate' working-class women in order to ensure that her home and family were managed more effectively. The relationship of one woman to another imbued with the authority that came from social superiority, was acclaimed as the medium through which such education would take effect.

As Gareth Steadman Jones (1971) points out: the exercise was undertaken out of fear of a class war. The Charity Organization Society was the logical complement to the reforms in London Poor Law administration that occurred at the end of the 1860s. There was a belief in the civilizing effects of personal relations between the classes. The practice of visiting the poor had been pioneered by the church and had been going on for a long time. Now, genteel ladies could extend not only sympathy but practical help, and attempt to remake the working class in a middle-class image.

However, this process had its contradictions. Any attempt by Victorian women to enter the public sphere – even when it complemented their domestic role – challenged the accepted position of women. Fears were expressed that those who became involved in welfare work would lose some of their womanly attributes – their submissiveness and adaptability. Therefore, alongside the exhortation to engage in philanthropic work, there were clear statements that women were only fitted for particular areas. These areas were designated by committees (usually composed of men) who claimed that it was important to ensure that women's essential qualities of enthusiasm, sympathy, self-sacrifice, and an eye for detail were steadied by the logic, business sense, and distance of men, who would be responsible for overall management. The iconography was of a perfectly matched husband and wife with a household and family to maintain. He was the head, and she the heart of the enterprise.

For women engaged in philanthropic work, the difficulties of realizing these ideals abounded. In their written accounts of work in settlements, Poor Law, and voluntary organizations, many women acknowledged the guilt that made communication with their undeserving sisters very difficult (Walton 1975). It was not just, as Wilson suggests, that the 'paradoxical situation' existed in which:

> 'middle-class women with no direct experience of marriage and motherhood themselves took on the social task of teaching marriage and motherhood to working-class women who were widely believed to be ignorant and lacking when it came to their domestic tasks.'
>
> (Wilson 1977)

It was also that the experiences of marriage and motherhood for upper- and middle-class women offered limited insights into the daily grind of women working and bringing up children for most of their adult lives, in overcrowded homes with no servants and little money. As the Hon. Mrs Arthur Lyttleton suggested in her chapter in the *Ladies Year Book* of 1901, 'It is sometimes difficult for women of a more educated class even to imagine the difficulties which beset the minds of the poor' (Lyttleton 1901:88).

In spite of these problems, welfare work continued to offer growing opportunities for female employment right up until the Second World War. In the middle class, the numbers of 'surplus women' increased after the slaughter of the First World War, and some of these women began to be drawn into such spheres as residential care, previously the domain of their working-class sisters.

Walton and Timms, among others, have shown the importance to middle- and upper-class women of the developing occupation of social work. As it grew they became active in instituting training of a professional kind for some branches of the work. It became apparent that there was a contradiction between the idea on the one hand that all that was required for social work were the natural caring attributes of women, and on the other hand that it needed something in the nature of specialized knowledge and skills that could be taught. This was partially (but never fully) resolved by classifying some areas of work as in need of more training than others. The areas that required training were those which exclusively recruited middle-class women – such as hospital almoning and psychiatric social work. Residential posts in this period still tended to be filled from the lower classes, who drew on their 'natural capacities' and therefore needed no training. This distinction between the two areas of work reflected a material consideration. Training was not free and cash grants were not available; therefore only women with independent means could be trained.

By this means the pattern that had begun to emerge in the nineteenth century, in which women from particular social backgrounds were drawn into particular spheres of work, was reinforced by the development of training, and social work became hierarchically structured in such a way that the trained élite of hospital almoners and psychiatric social workers was almost exclusively drawn from educated women of independent means (Walton 1975; Timms 1967).

The picture of the pre-war period is one in which it was 'men who were responsible for many of the creative initiatives, dominated committees and provided finance and support in the growing occupation of social work' (Walton 1975). The commitment and energies of their wives, sisters, daughters, and mothers were confined to specific levels of work that were designated as being compatible with their intrinsic qualities as women. These women – challenging male domination and pushing back the boundaries of their occupational confinement – appear to have been struggling with questions and pressures that had more to do with the fears they invoked in their male peers than the reactions to their activities at the front line. In fact, it is our view that debates within social work during this period concentrated on this issue, rather than questions of practice in relation to client need.

It is difficult to form a clear view without developing a much fuller picture of the experiences of the women at that time. In order to do this the existing histories need to be supplemented by the available accounts of women from the 'lower orders' who were both workers and clients. For example, the much criticized female Poor Law attendants who, it was argued, needed to be treated by lady visitors in the same way as household servants. Crucial to such accounts are the experiences of the women described in such surveys as Maud Pember Reeves' *Round About a Pound a Week* (Reeves 1913) and Margery Spring Rice's *Working Class Wives* (Spring Rice 1939). These are the women who were the recipients of the attentions of lady visitors, Poor Law officials, and almoners, when they became unable to continue the exhausting grind of work, child-bearing, and poverty.

The experience of the Second World War

The Second World War brought to light in a particularly dramatic way the relationship between women, the family, and welfare. The demands of total war and the necessary involvement of the civilian population resulted in women being called away from caring for their families in the home to work in industry, the services, and welfare (Titmuss 1950; Wilson 1977). As a result 'normal family life' was disrupted and the inadequacy of existing state and voluntary provision was exposed. The extent and cost of women's labour in the home was revealed and a restructuring and expansion of some areas of welfare took place, in which social workers came to play a crucial part.

As Angus Calder (1969) movingly demonstrates, the disruption among the wartime civilian population was on a scale difficult to conceive of nowadays. He describes the massive enterprise that was developed to tackle the problems of evacuation and billeting of women and children, and the immense resources of skill, tact, understanding, administration, and sympathy that must have been required. The existing welfare services, both voluntary and statutory, were not up to the job. It was during the war, therefore, that the health and welfare services started to standardize provision. The growing emergency – bombings, homelessness, orphans, and evacuation – meant that the means test became a bureaucratic impediment to supplying desperate and immediate needs and it began to disappear (Titmuss 1950). The beginnings of a *national* National Health Service could be seen as the voluntary hospitals were brought in to the state sector. Other areas of work were also opening up. The creation of

Citizens Advice Bureaux, the expansion of day nurseries to care for the children of working mothers, and work with the homeless were new areas demanding new skills and energies, and it was women who were called upon to organize and administer these services. Areas of social work thought of as traditionally male, for example, probation, were suffering from a dearth of male officers – and women were called upon to fill the gap.

These increased opportunities (both paid and unpaid) gave the chance for middle- and upper-class women to influence directly the policy and management of social work. But their entry into this sphere was often at a price. These women found (like women in industry) that their efforts were not considered to be worth the men's scale of remuneration.

The difficulties encountered in developing provision that met the needs of the consumers as well as the needs of the war effort were immense. Women, as both providers and recipients of such services, bore the brunt of living every day with these difficulties. The question of nursery care provides one pertinent example.

The number of day nursery places provided by the state in Britain during this period, in order to release women for production, has never been equalled. However, many women were unhappy about the *quality* of care given in nurseries. Lady Allen of Hurtwood, one of the influential figures in developing nursery provision at the time has written (1967) of the dilemmas she was placed in when she began to raise questions, not of provision but of the quality of that provision.

Lady Allen was a woman who had found the demands of family and career difficult to reconcile. She had had some pre-war involvement with the newly formed Nursery School Association and she had been struck by the difference this form of provision had made to working-class women. She noted how nursery classes enabled these women to: 'be freed for a few hours each day to get on with their housework and shopping and enjoy chats with their friends. They seemed to throw off their exhausted looks and become happier companions to their children and husbands' (Allen and Nicholson 1967:117). There is a quaintness in the notion that nurseries were a good thing because they enabled women to become better wives and mothers. But in the circumstances after the war when women were encouraged to rebuild the nation by devoting themselves entirely to their families, it was a notion that was quickly forgotten.

Lady Allen, among others, soon became aware that the Ministry of

Labour was not primarily interested in the welfare of children or mothers. Its main duty was to recruit more women to the factories. Of course, women with very young children were never conscripted, but they were urged to do war work and many of them welcomed the money, not to mention the new freedoms waged work brought. But for women with children, work was not an unmixed blessing. Part-time work was rarely available and full-time hours were long. Women wanting to work *and* spend some time with their children were frustrated. Children were taken to nursery and 'were asleep when they came in the early morning, and asleep when they went home' (Allen and Nicholson 1967:168).

Most of the women must have been concerned about their children and the time they spent in the grossly understaffed nurseries. Lady Allen attempted to demonstrate that the needs of babies from a few weeks old and those of children up to five years were being ineffectually met by inadequate numbers of staff whose training was brief and haphazard. Her estimates of the costs that would be incurred in staffing the nurseries she desired, led her to argue that it would be cheaper to pay women with children under two to stay at home! Not surprisingly, she received no response from government when she presented her evidence. When the war was over, the government, faced with the enormous cost of adequate socialized child care, quickly decided that young children were best cared for by their mothers and closed the majority of nursery places.

The public recognition of separate demands on women as mothers and as workers that became apparent during this period was not seen as consequential – one influencing and to an extent, determining the other. Rather, the two spheres of activity were firmly dichotomized. Motherhood was 'expressive', 'emotional', 'fulfilling', 'natural', and above all, personal. Hence, the pressures under which working women laboured were not seen as intimately connected with their position in the family, except in derogatory ways. The quality of mothering given by working women was often held up for public scrutiny and ridicule. Working when she had small children rendered the mother 'unnatural', 'uncaring', and 'selfish'. The fact that such mothers were putting in long hours at factories and offices, out of economic necessity (the war broke up many marriages), made no difference.

Of course, what the experience of evacuating and billeting children from large cities had revealed was not so much maternal deprivation but the consequences of generations of social and economic deprivation. Children were separated from their familiar social and material conditions in towns and cities and put into unfamiliar surroundings with people who might be unsympathetic or even hostile. Gross mistakes were made (Grafton 1982; Calder 1969; Titmuss 1950). Jack Rosenthal's play *The Evacuees* describes the experiences of two small Jewish boys in an unsympathetic Gentile household in which their normal cultural behaviour (e.g. not eating pork) is taken as evidence of *bad* behaviour. This is typical of the problems that arose. There was an outcry in the media from the 'respectable' recipients of poorer city children. This did not focus on the differences in economic backgrounds, but the rather more 'obvious inadequacy of parenting' among the urban workers. In the remedies developed by social workers to deal with bewildered children and hostile hosts we can detect the familiar habit of pinning responsibility for troubling conditions on deviant individuals.

It was from these wartime experiences that the development of post-war work with families took shape. There were: residential and rehabilitation centres for 'unbilletable' (perhaps ungrateful?) mothers and children; and the beginnings of the Family Service Unit in the form of a group of pacifists working 'side by side' with 'inadequate problem families'. The emphasis among social workers was to retrain:

> 'Families who, because of personal inadequacy and adverse circumstances have lost the will power, perhaps even the wish, to maintain normal standards of home and child care. Their lives are characterised by dirt, disintegration and disorder. They are often shiftless, apathetic and irresponsible to an almost incredible degree.'   (Younghusband 1947:77)

As men returned to the factories from the front the personal and public spheres, which had briefly begun to come together for a number of women during the war, were once again firmly separated. An ideological onslaught on working mothers was given some intellectual respectability with the publication of Bowlby's work on 'maternal deprivation' – a term that entered the common parlance of social workers and the public (Bowlby 1953). So began another attempt to remake working-class women along the lines of middle-class respectability; once more, social workers were the shock troops of the new battle. However, this time they had a new weapon – the post-war Welfare State.

Social work in the post-war period

The reconstruction of family life was a dominant theme in post-war welfare policies. Much of the 'welfare state' legislation of the Labour Government was based on popular (if mythological) assumptions about the nature of families and the pattern of duties and responsibilities between family members. As Wilson comments:

> 'The welfare state was certainly perceived as supportive of family life and was intended to ease the lot of the breadwinner and to improve the situation of his dependents. Yet it supported this particular form of family life – a breadwinner and dependents – simply because no one thought of any other way of doing things.'
>
> (Wilson 1980:16)

Success in rebuilding the family was seen as crucially dependent on women directing their time, interest, and energies as wives and mothers; to creating what Beveridge described as a 'proper domestic environment'. Consequently, it was through the family that the problems of child care which had been publicized in wartime Britain were to be tackled. The first priority, therefore, was to return women to the pre-war world in which home and paid work were alternative and separate spheres, both in conception and execution.

The response to all this from many women who had gained positions of influence in the world of welfare was a positive one. They were concerned at the destructive effect that the war had had on many families and they were quick to direct their efforts to a reinforcement of their idea of traditional family life.

When a Committee of Enquiry was set up in 1945 to examine state services for children 'deprived of a normal home life', a precedent was set. The Chair was taken by a woman, and half the membership of the committee were women. (The precedent was limited and final; women, after all, were experts on family life.) Through its findings and recommendations, the Curtis Committee reinforced the popular view that the best possible child care was provided by families, which meant, of course, mothers. It argued that where family care could not be provided the aim of welfare should be to 'reproduce the actual conditions of family life'. To this end they suggested that the state should provide family group homes in which groups comprising no more than twelve children of mixed age and sex would be cared for by a married couple. The husband would take full-time employment outside the home. Built into this new model of institutional care, therefore, was a relationship between men and women that reinforced an acceptance of low pay and status among women residential workers. After all, the main wage would be brought home by husbands (Davis 1981:37).

This cosy vision of state provision supporting normal family life was echoed in the report of the Subcommittee of the Womens Group on public welfare two years later (Womens Group: 1948). Concerned with the increase in child neglect which, it was supposed, had been generated by the war, the group suggested that one of the dominant characteristics of the families in these cases was the capacity of the mother: 'Frequently a family can survive in spite of a weak or vicious father; but it is rare that it can survive with an incapable mother, for it is she who is the coping stone of the structure.' (Womens Group: 1948).

From this analysis it followed that the problem of the neglected child had to be dealt with by strengthening 'the coping stone'. Social work intervention by means of casework or residential treatment, aimed at the 'moral rehabilitation' of mothers, was recommended.

The implications for women of this concern to re-establish normal family life were largely ignored. As Smart points out, in the immediate post-war period, 'the primary role of married women as home-makers and child rearers was legitimated in social security, health, tax and pension provisions' (Hutter and Williams 1981), and few voices were raised in protest at this. Those who did campaign against the proposition contained in the Beveridge Report – that women who were wives should be regarded as dependants – had no success in changing the status of married women in the new state benefit schemes (Abbott and Bompass 1943). Indeed, in the 1980s, this status continues to discriminate against women.

One of the consequences of the post-war development of welfare provision that emphasized the rebuilding of family life was an increased demand for social workers. Having proved their worth during the crisis of war, they were offered new career opportunities as local authorities, the probation service, and voluntary organizations expanded. There were few qualified social workers and because, traditionally, welfare organizations had depended on unqualified, educated women to fill posts, concern grew that the new services would be starved of recruits.

It was in response to these concerns that Eileen Younghusband produced two reports, in 1947 and 1951, which provided an overview of supply and demand for social work and made recommendations for training. The reports contain a fascinating portrait both of the state of social work during this period and of the changing demands being made on women social workers.

In the first report Younghusband adopted the feminine gender (as indeed the Curtis Report had done) when referring to social workers. This use, she argued, reflected the predominance of women in most branches of the occupation at that time. She went even further; many of these women, she claimed, had worked for years within extreme constraints imposed on them both by their working conditions and by the prevalent attitudes to working women.

'Because the professional social worker has developed her skill within the comparatively small voluntary organisation where little administrative experience could be gained and because she lays stress on the value of the individual service she performs, she finds herself left both with a range of responsibilities and a salary, neither of which significantly increases as the years pass by. She does not look forward to any post in which she will share in framing policy and administering a service, as might happen if she had entered the fields of medicine or education. It is perhaps significant that one writes of the social worker as "she" – that "she" who is alleged to have no dependents to support and to be happy to work for pin money because a sense of vocation would be killed by a decent salary.'

(Younghusband 1947:9)

Until such attitudes and conditions were changed, she argued, it was unlikely that the additional workers needed to staff the new services would be attracted. There was a lack of what she called 'professional plums' and this could prove a barrier to expanding the service. Her recommendations were: to extend training, develop career structures, and improve salaries. This was not just to improve the lot of social workers, but, more importantly, to attract *men* into the service – men who, she pointed out, would not be content to start at 'the same salary as a good shorthand typist'.

Following the creation of the National Health Service and local

authority welfare and children's departments, Younghusband up-
dated her report in 1951. There was however, a significant change.
Instead of the concern over the plight of the woman social worker, the
emphasis had shifted radically so that her *primary* concern was for
attracting men to the service. Interestingly, the feminine gender was
dropped (and has never been used since in an equivalent document)
and instead of the contributions of women, it was the problems they
posed that were emphasized.

It had become Eileen Younghusband's opinion that: 'many married women find it almost impossible to combine the long hours of full
time employment with household demands and shopping difficulties'. Nor was part-time work an answer – the nature of the job,
especially in casework, demanded that 'the personal relationship
between the worker and the person in need are of the essence of the
work and cases do not confine themselves to the days or hours when
the worker is available' (1951:45). Men, according to this logic, were
therefore a much more reliable source of recruitment. They did not
suffer from 'the marriage and family responsibilities mortality which
decimates the ranks of women social workers within a few years of
training'. However, while competition for training places was stiff,
many men were still deterred from joining the profession by the low
salaries being offered in parts of the service. If only, she argued,
conditions could be improved, it would then be possible to recruit
large numbers of men in a way that would both meet the demands for
staff and overcome the traditional dependence on women.

Significantly the shift in emphasis between these two reports
reflects a change that was taking place in the relationship between
women and social work. In the pre-war period, social work (excepting
some areas of the probation service) had been seen as the natural
province of unmarried women and married women who had money
enough to have help in the house. During the war the work of such
women had enhanced the status of social work in general. But the
post-war expansion and institutionalization of this work coincided
with a dwindling number of unmarried women; a climate in which
married women were being encouraged to stay at home; and finally, a
disappearance of the servant class who had freed middle-class women
from domestic work (Wilson 1980:21). Hence the emphasis on
attracting men.

It was particularly ironic that at a time when the activities of social workers were focusing on the family, some women were being drawn out of social work precisely because of the kind of family responsibilities that in Younghusband's view undoubtedly added 'to the workers' understanding of those whose entanglements frequently centre round the same matters'. The 1950s was a decade in which the establishment of stable family life was looked to as a means of preventing the growth of a whole range of social problems. A woman's presence in the home was seen as an essential ingredient of this stability, and the expanding army of social workers and health visitors was exhorted to play a key role in supporting it.

When Younghusband in her first report identified the two most prominent problems faced by social workers in the aftermath of war, she pinpointed 'the precocious, overdeveloped, highly sexed adolescent girl, the "good time" girl, craving for excitement' and the 'problem family' (Younghusband 1947:62). As Smart shows, these were to remain prime concerns in the world of welfare throughout the subsequent decade. They were not only reflected in the moral intervention of social workers, but also in the legal developments of the mid-1950s that focused on the sexuality of young women (Hutter and Williams 1981:56).

There were important changes taking place in recruitment to the service over the period 1951–61. Men were gaining significantly from the provision of state grants for training; male recruits to managerial positions doubled in relation to the proportion of women in these posts (Walton 1975:222). Women, as Hubback's study revealed, were finding it harder to return to social work after marriage – even at basic-grade level. For instance, the part-time posts that were available in other occupations, such as nursing, teaching, and medicine, did not exist (Hubback 1957:105). The arguments being used against the introduction of part-time social work were that successful social work required continuity, long hours, and an emotional commitment that could not be supplied on anything but a full-time basis.

The problems that women social workers were having in reconciling family commitments and career were echoed in a different form in the lives of the women who became social work clients. The prevailing view, that the Welfare State had alleviated poverty, did not reflect the experiences of many women clients during this period. Faced with poor incomes they were caught in a classic trap. If they did not work they could not support their families on the inadequate level of state benefits. And if they chose to work in order to provide an adequate family wage, they were at risk of being seen as neglectful mothers by social workers, who had absorbed Bowlby's ideas about the crucial importance of the mother–child relationship.

'Latch-key' children were seen as an overwhelming social problem, to be tackled by dissuading the mothers from working outside the home, rather than providing more adequate child care services. Some of the gains won by women during the war were being steadily eroded as they were pushed back into the home. Those who could not afford to give up work turned to other women in their family and neighbourhood to give them the help with their children that the state chose not to provide.

The emphasis on the sanctity of family life did not just have implications for women with children. As the residential programmes, launched in 1948 for the care of the growing numbers of elderly people, were cut back, female relatives (married and unmarried) found themselves caring for those who became handicapped in old age. Few commentators at that time acknowledged the dominance of women amongst the elderly population (Titmuss 1958:10). Yet the majority of these women found themselves having to manage on subsistence incomes that reflected a lifetime of low status in the labour market.

The 1960s

The 1960s saw an emphasis on 'professionalization'. There was the beginning of a home-grown casework literature (Timms 1964) and a growing number of social work courses and departments in universities. Although some areas of social work had already established professional credentials – probation, medical social work, and child care – concern was expressed about the lack of such professionalism in other areas. At long last, residential care was drawn into this arena. Many of those who argued that this form of work suffered from a poor image lay the blame on those women who had been the mainstay of the residential services. It was their personal attributes, rather than any structural causes, that were holding back the professionalization of this work.

Some of the papers presented at the 1965 Annual Review of the Residential Child Care Association ('Change and the Child in Care') capture this tendency well. Wicks, in a discussion of the growth of professionalism stated:

> 'To care for the children "in care" in the sixties, we do not seek only the warm motherly type, filled with emotional "gush" for the "poor dear children", we seek the humane, gay, tolerant, sensible men and women of good intelligence, who can have their natural abilities trained to do therapeutic work with hard, bitter, aggressive, vulgar and unappreciative children. The kind of men and women we need with the ambition to do worthwhile work on behalf of the community are available but the image of the house–parent, as a glorified domestic or a warm, buxom, motherly type is repellent to them and often they seek to achieve their ambitions and satisfy their sense of vocation in other ways.'   (RCCA 1965)

Wicks was contrasting what he clearly thought were male and female styles of care – to the detriment of the female. Women were amateur and emotional in their approach to child care. To be professional depended on a partnership between men and women. This was not all; the basis of that partnership had a familiar ring, in that it mirrored the relationship between men and women that was an intrinsic part of family life. Men were 'rational' and women 'emotional', therefore it was self-evident that men should take the important decisions and direct women's work.

Nevertheless, there was some failure of nerve. Henry, in a paper that dealt with 'The Man in Residential Child Care' took on the vexing question of whether this kind of work was unnatural for men. In answering it he argued that there were qualities that men could bring to this kind of work, for example:

> 'the ease with which most men can handle a quarrelsome group of children and in dealing with an issue before it reaches an unreasonable proportion, preserve the womenfolk from the more arduous disciplinary duties which they in any case find more difficult and retain them for those elements of the job, tenderness, warmth, understanding, comfort, sympathy, which though not exclusively a female province they nevertheless do extremely well.'   (RCCA 1965)

Official approval was given to this 'opening up' of a predominantly female preserve in the Williams Committee Report of 1967. The committee pointed to the traditional dependence of all branches of this service on unmarried women who had been prepared to devote their lives to the work. It noted that the growth in the number of small residential units had coincided with dwindling reserves of unmarried women. Staff shortages of worrying proportions, it asserted, would be the result. The way forward was to provide the specialist training and career structure that would attract individuals with knowledge and skills to replace 'the motherly women or the economical housekeeper' who had been seen as the backbone of the service in the past. In this way, the stage was set for similar (though smaller scale) developments to take place, as had been seen in fieldwork in the previous decade. Increasing numbers of men were to secure management positions in a service where women still predominated at the front line.

The contrasts made between the 'old' and the 'new' in the residential field were also echoed in the expanding territory of community work at the end of the decade. As Elizabeth Wilson suggests, the comparisons made in this area were between women and the out-moded, and men and the future. Here, 'the image was of a long-haired young man, recently a student, opposed to dowdy conservative PSW or almoner, the Young Turks against the old maids' (Mayo 1977:9).

As for the probation service, 1967 saw the end of the situation in which male officers were prohibited from supervising female probationers. Phyllida Parsloe's 1969 study of probation officers' case-loads reveals an astonishing picture of the fears that this change engendered in those working in the service. Many expressed the view that male officers were being placed in a vulnerable position, not only exposed to sexual overtures from their deviant female clients, but also having to deal with their own feelings of sexual attraction towards such women. Female officers, it would appear, were not subject to the same risk. After all, in adopting a caring but authoritative attitude towards their clients (male or female), they were fitting into the asexual stereotype of the 'normal, good mother' (Parsloe 1972).

As for women's experiences as clients during this period, state concerns about family life underwent a change in emphasis. A major focus was on problems of delinquency, the causes of which were linked to problems of family and community disintegration. An increase in divorce rates and growing numbers of mothers engaging in employment outside the home were both cited as causes of the rise in juvenile crime. So too was the disappearance of traditional communities and the extended family, both changes which, it was claimed, exposed the handicapped and elderly to neglect and isolation. Here the planners could be blamed; but often, in contact with the welfare services, women found themselves being held responsible for their failure to make good the consequences of these changes.

Fears that the family and the community were 'no longer what they used to be' did not result in a lessening of the demands on both to care for more of their members. The move away from institutional care for elderly, mentally ill, and mentally handicapped people that began in the 1960s was in general hailed as a progressive move. But the under funding of the whole exercise was ignored. Part of the burden of care was being shifted away from paid workers and placed on the shoulders of relatives, friends, volunteers – anyone with a developed sense of guilt – and the majority of these groups faced with new responsibilities were women (Hunt 1968).

The Seebohm Report (1968) was the major government initiative in response to the range of problems that clients presented for social workers during this period. The report argued for the creation of a unified local authority department, providing a community-based family service. This gave organizational expression to the dominant welfare concerns of the decade. The argument was that an increase in the size of social service departments would provide a more effective and beneficial service to its users. As a result, clients found themselves confronted with another large, impersonal welfare bureaucracy.

Social work post-Seebohm

The consequences for women social workers of the creation of local authority social service departments have not received much attention. The issues that have been focused on have been the implications of bureaucratization for the profession, ignoring the fact that the experiences of women employed in the new departments were not identical to those of men. The appointment of directors of the new departments in 1970–71 demonstrated a further loss of managerial control by women. Prior to 1970 a fifth of all local authority chief officer appointments in England and Wales were women (mainly in child care departments). On this basis, it could have been assumed that between thirty and forty women might have been appointed to head the new departments. In fact only fourteen women were appointed to the 160 available posts (Walton 1975:236). This pattern was reflected throughout the new management structures, with the minority of women who were appointed placed in second- and third-tier managerial levels. In other words, they tended to fill professional adviser and training officer posts. The situation in 1984 had worsened slightly for women, with 12 out of the 120 directors' posts in England and Wales being filled by women.

The gains of the reorganization for women workers were in traditional female skills posts: an expansion in secretarial, home-help, social work assistant, and residential care posts offered women more opportunities, but in very limited fields. Significantly, there was a breakthrough in the availability of part-time social work. Hall and Hall's study (1980) suggests that from the early 1970s there was 'a steady and substantial real increase' in the number of part-time social workers employed in local authority departments and hospitals. By 1977 they estimate that part timers (97 per cent being women) represented 15 per cent of fieldwork staff in English social service departments. Most of these were unqualified and therefore engaged in the more 'menial social work tasks'.

The post-Seebohm debates did not touch on this further consolidation of managerial power by male workers. Instead they focused on what appeared to be an increasing questioning of traditional social work and attempts to politicize social work activities. This development has been described in the professional literature as a turning away from concerns about work with the individual and a turning towards concerns about the social, political, and economic issues that affect exchanges between workers and clients. Out of the wealth of material on this theme, what has interested us is the part that women workers were seen as playing in the emergence of radical critiques of social work. In general, no distinction is made between the experiences of men and women workers in relation to the political debates within social work. This is true of all parties to the debate, whatever their political allegiances. On the left, for example, *Case Con* did not see any reason to produce an issue on women until 1974 – four years after the emergence of the Women's Movement in this country. It is only in explanations of the growth of Radical Social Work that we find male/female distinctions being drawn, and then in a manner that is hardly complimentary to women. Radical Social Work emerged, many have claimed, as a reaction to the old-style, female-dominated casework tradition, and as a consequence of the new-style political and male-dominated social work of the 1970s.

John Cypher, in his contribution to a book that saw the crisis and questioning in social work as a positive development, expounded this theme at some length as he charted the relationship between social work reform and the social work profession. He saw the emergence of radical activists in the early 1970s as the consequence of a new type of individual entering the profession: they were 'male (or female with masculine traits) of middle-class origin, possessors of a university social science degree and somewhat younger than others in the profession' (Jones 1975:21). Cypher's reasoning here is interesting, in that he sees the profession as traditionally offering opportunities to women who, when they:

> 'enter the work place are attracted to those occupations like social work that emphasise interpersonal communications, empathy, subjectivity and nurturance. Such occupations are traditionally filled by women because of the personal qualities derived from femininity and reinforced by socialisation that women possess.'
>
> (Jones 1975:16)

Such individuals, he explains, tend to be passive and not interested in change, reform, or militancy, 'they may even resist such developments or leave them to men and to women with the required masculine traits'. The other group attracted to social work in the post-war period have been men from working-class backgrounds for whom the profession offers a prospect of upward mobility. They too, according to Cypher, are unlikely to bite the hand that feeds them. The activists, therefore, are a minority and an untypical group, up against a conservative and individually focused tradition within the profession, fostered by women and working-class men!

This assessment of the inherent passivity and conservative nature of women social workers, at a time when the Women's Movement was a growing force in Britain, offers an insight into the slowness with which social work has absorbed the ideas and practice emerging from feminism. It was in this very period that women campaigned successfully for changes relating to women's lives – especially in the areas of pay, work opportunities, abortion, domestic violence, and less successfully, social security. At the same time, the Women's Movement

LIBRARY
College of St. Francis
JOLIET, ILLINOIS

123,545

was responsible for developing services for women who had been raped or battered. These took place in parallel to the largely statutory practice of social workers and had limited impact on the theory taught on training courses.

The debates of the early seventies about the politicization of social work have shifted direction with the restructuring of welfare provision that has taken place in Britain since the mid-1970s. This change of context has resulted in the occupation of social work becoming increasingly defensive – justifying its efforts and continued existence. This new climate in welfare places increased pressure on women working in the state and voluntary sectors, and on women clients.

Effecting savings and cutting back on welfare expenditure at a time of growing unemployment has reinforced the message that women should be providing more care for those who need it. With fewer resources to offer individuals in difficulty, women welfare workers find themselves expected to seek out and use informal networks to meet crises: that is to say, other women in the family and community (NISW (Barclay Report) 1982). Persuading women to put the needs of their children, handicapped and elderly relatives and friends, before their own, can place women social workers in the position of reinforcing patterns of domestic existence that they personally have questioned and tried to reject. In such situations it is difficult to refute Miles' (1981) claim that 'women social workers are aiding their own oppression by oppressing women clients'.

The rewards offered by the state to women who are prepared to care for others have not increased as demand for their services expands. Indeed, in Britain married and cohabiting women who stay at home to look after a disabled person are not allowed to claim the invalid care allowance which is available to men and single women who provide the same care to others (EOC 1981).

Similarly, the financial rewards given to women working in the voluntary sector, who provide much needed services to such groups as battered and raped women, are sparse. The state uses their energies and commitment to provide low cost responses to women in need.

For many women in Britain in the early 1980s the pressures of managing the financial, physical, social, and psychological repercussions of growing unemployment are formidable. Not only are they faced with dwindling opportunities to work and earn themselves (Haringey and Lewisham Women's Employment Project 1981), but

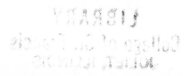

they are struggling to contain the tensions generated in their own homes by others for whom they feel responsible. In such circumstances it is inevitable that their chances of finding themselves in a social work encounter increase.

In this situation it is our belief that the ideas developed by feminists, ideas that do not divorce the political from the personal, and that locate the situation of women in the ambivalent stance that the state takes to the family, offer the richest source of understanding for women welfare workers and women clients in the 1980s.

2

The unitary approach: a feminist critique

MARY LANGAN

Introduction

Women who receive the attention of social workers have always been those who are most oppressed – in terms of low income and the burdens of family life. From the workhouse to the women's refuge, women afflicted by their position in society have become social work clients. Today most of the activities begun by nineteenth-century philanthropists have been taken over by state-employed social workers. Although most social work clients and most social workers are women, the theory and practice of social work reflect little appreciation of the important questions of women's oppression.

Social work in Britain began its second post-war boom in the early 1970s, just as the British economy began its plunge into the deepest recession for fifty years. As the state overhauled its mechanisms for dealing with the poor, the unemployed, and the disadvantaged, the social work profession grew in size and status. The Seebohm Report (1968) encouraged the establishment of local authority social services departments that brought together a wide range of welfare provisions under the direction of teams of 'generic' social workers.

Social work theory does not just provide an intellectual and research-based foundation for the discipline traditionally derived from medicine, psychiatry, and psychoanalysis; it exists to rationalize social work practice and to enhance the precarious status of the profession (Jones 1979). In the wake of the reorganization of social work in the early 1970s, a new synthesis of traditional theories with modern social science concepts emerged to give the diverse functions of the new generic social worker some coherence. The 'unitary approach' or 'unitary method' (sometimes called the 'integrated methods approach') was the result. It remains a popular model for the theory and practice of social work.

The unitary approach has received very little evaluation or criticism from women's point of view. The only feminist contribution to date is by Dominelli and McLeod (1982). This is surprising because the unitary approach embodies all the prevalent conservative assumptions and prejudices about women's role in society. A 1976 survey of popular social work texts in use on CQSW courses reveals how much of the literature accepts uncritically the dominant ideologies surrounding women's role – at work, in child-bearing and child-rearing, and in sexual relations (Waller 1976). The unitary method provides the rationale for the further incorporation of such ideologies in social work practice. So a feminist critique of the unitary method is long overdue.

Professionals in search of a theory

Up to the Second World War, welfare workers sought to alleviate the extremes of want and distress, while reinforcing the values of hard work and moral virtue, temperance and thrift (see chapter 1). Despite the evident relationship between destitution and the fluctuations of the capitalist economy from the mid-nineteenth century onwards, the doctrine of individual moral culpability for poverty was dominant. The best guarantor of the interests of the poor, according to conventional wisdom, was the free operation of market forces. The poor could and should be assisted, but only by means that did not remove their incentive to work or weaken the profit motive in the provision of basic amenities, such as decent housing.

Dramatic changes occurred after the Second World War. Through rearmament and reconstruction the state interfered in the free market to enforce a major rationalization of the economy. These changes ushered in the longest crisis-free period in the history of British capitalism. The endemic mass unemployment of the 1920s and 1930s disappeared, and with it much of the gross deprivation and demoralization of the inter-war years. Government intervention stabilized the economy and, through the reorganization of education, health, and welfare services, claimed to have created the framework for the abolition of poverty and all its attendant evils.

However, poor housing, low income, and delinquency persisted throughout the 1950s and 1960s. In part, these problems were attributed to the bureaucratic inefficiency of the various welfare agencies in ensuring adequate provision for particular needs. But it was the problem family – the modern version of individual responsibility for poverty – that got most of the blame. Through its inadequate performance of basic family functions and its incompetence in obtaining welfare entitlements, the problem family was found guilty of perpetuating a cycle of deprivation.

By the late 1960s it had become apparent that social problems could no longer be reduced to minor technical malfunctions and a few incorrigible families. Sociologists rediscovered poverty (Townsend and Able-Smith 1965). The reorganization of 'National Assistance' as 'Supplementary Benefits' in 1966 reflected the government's recognition that the section of society receiving the state's subsistence pay-outs, expected to decline to insignificance in the 1950s, was set for a major and lasting expansion.

The crisis of the late 1960s provided the context for the major reorganization and expansion of social work. State intervention in the economy had become both more extensive and more widely accepted since the war; now the state moved beyond its role in social security, health, education, and housing to deal systematically with the problems of poverty through the provision of 'family and community services'.

Social work as a profession was weak and fragmented before 1970. Although the majority of social workers were employed by local government, many worked alongside the state services in a variety of voluntary and charitable bodies. In the local authority services there were child care officers, mental health officers, and welfare officers responsible for the care of the elderly and disabled. The supervision of problem families was divided among these officials and a variety of other Welfare State agencies. The Seebohm Report in 1968 led to a major rationalization of these diverse services. This, together with the Children and Young Persons Act 1969, the Chronically Sick and Disabled Persons Act 1970, and the Children Act 1975, legitimized the extension of social workers' powers over children, the mentally ill, and over a range of tasks previously carried out by the police, probation officers, rent or debt collectors, public assistance officers, sanitary inspectors, and electricity boards (Jordan 1977). All these tasks were united in the person of the generic social worker, and social work as a profession appeared to come of age.

The diverse functions and traditions within the new local authority social services departments were reflected in the disparate character of the generic social workers' theories and methods. There were broadly three different approaches: casework, groupwork, and community work. All sought to incorporate psychological and sociological theories from the relevant academic disciplines in order to give their work some legitimacy and status.

Casework appropriated psychoanalytic theories along with its existing patriarchal biases. It enjoyed widespread popularity in the 1950s and 1960s as it corresponded with the prevailing vogue for individualizing social problems. People were poor and under-privileged because they were personally inadequate, the victims of defective upbringing and residual childhood complexes. Social workers could claim a distinct skill in working with deviant individuals, especially in preventing breakdowns. Although there has been a move away from psychoanalytic casework, notions of individual or family pathology as the root of social problems remain influential in contemporary social work.

Feminists have seen the potential of psychoanalysis in various ways – some contradictory. (These views are explored further by Davis, Llewelyn, and Parry in Chapter 4.) What has happened in casework theory, however, is that the anti-female assumptions within psychoanalysis have remained unexamined and have been incorporated into this form of social work practice.

Group work emerged from Klein's development of Freudian concepts in relation to group behaviour. This approach was broadened in the 1960s to include newer psychological theories – behaviour therapy, transactional analysis, and learning and communication theory.

Community work was a response to the growth of tenants groups, consumer associations, and pressure groups of various social minorities. It used sociological research to develop techniques for tackling social pathology at the community level. This approach was seen in its most sophisticated form in the early 1970s with the launching of the central government sponsored Community Development Project.

This programme, described by the Home Office as 'a radical experiment in community development', was based on action research. It demonstrated that solutions to the problems experienced in local communities needed change at the highest levels of the political structure. In Saltley, for example, one of the unexpected problems presented by some residents to the project workers was that they could not buy their freeholds, although they had a legal right to do so. Intervention by the project staff revealed that this problem was insurmountable. The freeholders were owners of capital who would not relinquish the freeholds without lengthy and expensive legal battles, which the residents could not afford. In Saltley the conclusion was reached that neighbourhood work could not resolve problems that had 'deep-seated structural causes' that lay 'outside our neighbourhood – in our system of wealth and property' (Lees and Smith 1975:90). The Community Development Project was a brave attempt to address social problems in terms of poverty and deprivation by mobilizing communities. The evidence emerging about the limits to this kind of intervention was uncomfortable to governments of any political persuasion and the initiative was terminated in 1974.

Seebohm promoted the integration of a whole range of different social work activities, under the control of a single local authority department staffed by social workers capable of dealing with any social problems from a battered baby to a neighbourhood campaign for a zebra crossing. While Seebohm (1968) rationalized social work in practice, Pincus and Minahan (1977), Goldstein (1973), Specht (1977), and Vickery (1977), among others, set about rationalizing the chaos of existing social work theory. The unitary method was the result.

Building the model

The architects of the unitary approach were explicit about the professional ambitions behind their theoretical constructions. According to Pincus and Minahan (1977:104): 'It hopefully represents a reformulation of the base of social work practice which gives social work a clear place among the human service professions.' Carving out a place for the social work profession meant borrowing bits of theory from the other 'human service' professions. For Goldstein (1977:68) this was nothing to be ashamed of as 'it is a given fact that social work is dependent on the social and behavioural sciences for substantive knowledge and in no way does this fact detract from the integrity of the profession'.

The unitary approach took shape from pieces of 'substantive knowledge' derived from the social sciences. Pincus and Minahan explain how they set about producing the unitary method:

> 'In developing our model we began by examining the tasks of the social worker in action as he [sic] works to change elements in a social situation in order to achieve a specific goal or outcome. Our model grew by bits and pieces as we isolated and identified basic elements in practice that were reflected in these tasks. We borrowed from existing formulations in the literature.'
>
> (Pincus and Minahan 1977:73)

The 'existing formulations' that Pincus and Minahan acknowledge were derived from systems theory. This highly developed and much criticized approach has been prevalent in the social sciences for some time and had been applied to a variety of areas, particularly industrial management.

For Goldstein (1977:68), this approach could be combined with an enthusiasm for empirical testing: 'the particular task and contribution of the profession was the ability to integrate these pieces of knowledge, transform them into operational strategies and test their validity for the resolution of social problems.'

All three authors were building a model rooted in a theory that had emerged as part of what Mishra (1983:9) describes as 'the dominant social theory of the two post-war decades' – functionalism. Talcott Parsons' work on the theory of structural functionalism made the major contribution here. For Parsons the concept of 'system' was fundamental to understanding the structure and function of society. To understand the nature of a system Parsons drew an analogy with an organism. An organism was an example of a system and as such displayed two important characteristics. First, an interdependence of its 'parts', and second a tendency for these parts to maintain an 'equilibrium' in their relationship to each other.

Parsons' work on social systems emphasized their inherent stability. In other words, for Parsons, 'How is order possible?' was a more important question than 'How can change occur?'. This focus brought with it a preoccupation with the moral values that produce and maintain order, and this deeply conservative stance runs through all of Parsons' writing.

There are problems in using this approach to understand the world of social work. Take, for example, a family in which the wife and mother is being regularly beaten by her husband. For Parsons this would be an extreme reflection of normal family life, dependent for its equilibrium on a dominant (and 'instrumental') father and a submissive (and 'expressive') mother. The way to treat or re-adjust this system would be, presumably, some sort of psychological therapy directed at the couple. Its purpose would be to maintain the stability of the family. Feminists would see this problem as one inherent in the nature of marriage and the family in a patriarchal society (Wilson 1983). The system that reinforces a woman's economic and emotional dependence on her husband makes it difficult for her to choose to leave him if she is to maintain herself and her children. The same system imposes the role of patriarch and breadwinner on a husband, and not all men find it easy to conform to this expectation.

However, Goldstein (1973:110) maintains that systems theory 'provides a framework for gaining an appreciation of the entire range of elements that bear on a social problem including the social units involved, their expansive and dynamic characteristics, their interrelations and the implications for change in one as it affects all others'. In fact, social systems theory is not so much a framework for the unitary approach, as its body work – a slick finish that renders its eclecticism virtuous. As Pincus and Minahan (1977) concede, 'the model is not based on any substantive communication theory or conflict resolution, but allows for the selective incorporation of such theoretical orientations in working with specific situations'.

Society viewed through the spectacles of the systems theorists is simply an assembly of individuals in various sized units, all interacting in mutual harmony within the system as a whole. Malfunctions in the system can only occur at the interfaces between the boxes: the boxes themselves, being empty, contain no sources of conflict.

However, is this model really adequate? Individuals are divided by class and gender: their relations are characterized by oppression and resistance, domination and conflict. They are neither harmonious nor constant. Women have not always suffered the oppression of family life in its modern form. The changing positions of workers and of women result from the different ways different societies are organized, not from any laws of nature. The key point is that society was not always ordered in the past as it is in the present, nor need it be so ordered in the future. Unitary approach theorists make no attempt to understand or change the world: their fundamental assumption is that it will stay more or less the same. They avoid discussion of exploitative relationships.

The ahistorical concepts of the unitary approach and its presumption of accepted moral values and social harmony obscure social conflict while upholding existing power relations. A clear example of this is in the notion that the family should provide care for all its members, in particular the very young, the very old, and those who are disabled. In discussions about what family care comprises, there would be no analysis, from a unitary perspective, of the exploitative relationships that exist within the family. The accepted moral value that 'family is best', which is currently being reinforced by government policies of community care, would be upheld, yet the success of community care, measured in terms of the closure of state residential provision, is dependent on the willingness of women as relatives, friends, and neighbours to work in an unpaid capacity, caring for others. Women who take on this kind of caring often put the needs of others before their own. They live with the effects of repetitive hard work and isolation. They experience conflict in a number of ways. Often they find themselves in conflict with other family members who do not take on an equal share of the caring. They are in regular and painful conflict with those they care for, when demands for care and attention are felt to be oppressive. They are in conflict with themselves, for in deciding to care, often for years on end, they lose opportunities to pursue other interests. But these aspects of family care and community care are never part of the unitary agenda. The focus is on the solutions that the family or community can provide to a range of social problems. Social problems indicate a local malfunction: social work aims to restore the balance.

The unitary approach has gained popularity among some social workers, but particularly among social work educators. For them the unitary approach has provided a symbolic ordering of the messy reality of social work practice. It has enabled them to overcome the fragmentation of social work in the 'tri-method approach' (casework, group work, and community work) by integrating all the various ways of understanding social work into a single model. It has provided a welcome alternative to the pursuit of increasingly esoteric theories of individual and group behaviour.

An important additional reason for the acceptance of the unitary approach, especially among students, is its claim that it transcends the traditional focus of social work on the individual client. The move beyond the exclusive client focus to include a greater recognition of the community and other social and state institutions has given the unitary approach a certain radical appeal. Even a left-wing critic of the unitary approach can identify this aspect of the approach as potentially progressive. Leonard (1975), for example, accepting the empty boxes of the social systems theorists, considers that these boxes can be filled with a progressive content and the unitary approach operated in a radical manner. However, this reduces the conservative element in the unitary approach to the possibility of the boxes having an 'oppressive' rather than 'supportive' content. But the fundamental problem with the unitary approach is the whole notion of interacting boxes, assuming a biological model for the operation of society. It is the basic assumptions of the unitary approach that render it useless for understanding or changing society, not the particular pieces of theory it appropriates in relation to a particular social problem. In fact, the unitary method's recognition of the broader social factors that impinge on an individual client is neither new nor radical: it simply indicates a more sophisticated way of reconciling individuals to an oppressive social reality, and this cannot be used by feminists or the left.

Because this approach assumes that the boxes of a social system do interrelate in a manner that maintains equilibrium, it makes nonsense of the model to replace a box labelled 'wife' with one labelled 'independent woman'. This substitution of boxes to reflect a feminist view of what might be, immediately throws the model into contradiction. Such a contradiction can only be resolved by destroying the underlying principles of stability and equilibrium – by getting rid of the organic analogy.

For Goldstein (1977:68–70) the virtue of systems theory was 'the way that it simultaneously offered a view of order, relation and effect when applied to a social phenomenon'; the aim of the social worker in dealing with those out of step with the status quo is 'to foster change and at the same time attend to the conditions which permit that system to retain enough equilibrium to manage that change'. What exactly does this mean? The key is in the word 'system'. Systems range in size from the individual, to the family, to the school, and a local authority social services department. If the word 'individual' or 'mother' or 'family' is substituted for the word 'system', we can see the profound conservatism of this approach. Change is permissible within the system but not within the structure, because the system has to harmonize with the structure.

The assumption is that it is beneficial to restore the client's relationship with the existing system to structural equilibrium, whether by some minor adjustment in their outlook or their circumstances. This is the crux of the matter for feminists, because for women, the whole problem is that the patriarchal equilibrium of modern society is profoundly disadvantageous to their interests. Adjustments in outlook or circumstance, in order to maintain or restore the status quo, enmeshes women more deeply in a world that exploits and oppresses them. It is in challenging and changing the balance of forces within society that women can begin to fulfil themselves.

Trapped in the systems

The feminist critique of the unitary method emerges out of the general analysis of the position of women in society that has been developed in the women's movement. Feminists have challenged prevailing assumptions about women's role and have exposed the structurally subordinate position of women within all the major institutions of society. These very assumptions – about women's inferior position in the labour market, about their privatization in the family – are accepted by the unitary method and reinforced by its operation in social work practice.

The fact that women form the bulk of social work clients is more fruitfully seen as a consequence of the intense pressures on women, resulting from their inferior position as wage workers outside the family and as domestic workers inside the family, than from an imbalance within an existing system of equilibrium. Women's marginal position in the labour market condemns them to greater poverty, dependence on men, state benefits, and more oppressive working conditions. Women suffer higher levels of unemployment and are concentrated in the most backward sections of the economy where they endure low wages, long hours, and poor facilities. Home workers, the most exploited of all wage earners, are almost exclusively female. At the same time, as is all too well known, women generally bear the burden of work in the home. They look after men, the children, the sick, and the elderly; they do the cooking, the cleaning, and the shopping. Housework reinforces women's subordinate position in society. The home as a private sphere accentuates women's isolation and dependence. It is not surprising that social workers are often required to cope with the breakdown of this system (single parent families, delinquent children, non-accidental injury, rent and fuel bill arrears, etc.).

For the theorists of the unitary method, the family is another social unit like the individual and the community, with its own internal dynamics and external equilibrium with the rest of society. The family is an interacting system which serves the needs of its individuals in dynamic interaction with one another. The role of the social worker is to intervene to preserve and restore the balance of the system.

'The worker may be seeking to help family members to change the way they relate to each other, to help them provide emotional support and affection for one another . . . the worker's activities are directed towards helping individual members of the system carry out their roles within the system as well as improving the operation of the system as a whole.'   (Pincus and Minahan 1977:76)

The unitary method treats the family as a natural, biological, and essentially harmonious unit. But feminist critiques have shown that the family is historically a specific form of social organization that reproduces and reinforces patriarchal power relations. Unitary method social work seeks to preserve and perpetuate the key institution maintaining women's oppression. Improving the operation of the system is of little benefit to women when the system as a whole operates to reproduce their subordination.

The notion of the dynamic interaction of the family welfare system disguises the structural subordination of women and the ideologies that reinforce it. Women's capacity to work is limited by their position in the family, their dependence on men, and their responsibility for domestic work. At the same time the family is the sphere in which gender socialization takes place. Masculine responsibility and authority, feminine passivity and maternity are constituted in the family.

The unitary method attributes family problems to the malfunctioning of the system – little advance on the problem family thesis of the 1950s. Straightening out the deviant family and its deviant members may now be called family therapy, and it may be disguised in systems theory language, but the basic approach shows little change since the Second World War: 'The goal of family therapy is to change role relations in the family in such a way as to free individuals from having to engage in pathologically induced and supported role behaviour' (Vickery 1977:129).

The concept of the family that guides orthodox social work today takes the specific form of the nuclear family and makes it into a universal ideal. The ideal presumes a male breadwinner, a female dependent housewife, and a small number of children. However, recent research has revealed that such families are scarce. It has been shown that the number of households that conform to this stereotype is small (Land 1976; Rapaport and Fogarty 1982). A Study Commission on the Family report (Rimmer 1981) recognized that the notion of the nuclear family comprising two natural parents and their legitimate children bears little relation to the typical British family. Only one third of households comprise such families, and only 15 per cent conform to the image of mother at home and father as breadwinner. The report noted that 10 per cent of children are illegitimate; one in five children is likely to witness parental divorce. Marriage is on the decline, cohabitation on the increase. About one in eight children live in one-parent families. While the family may be a minority institution, family ideology embraces all. Nowhere is this contradiction more stark than among social work clients where the ideal family is as rare as a wealthy woman. Yet most social workers' practice is informed by the prevailing assumptions about the normal family and the need to conserve it. As Dominelli and McLeod point out:

'Working with families is a main area of social work intervention. And it is the way in which social workers handle family situations and the assumptions behind their practice that constitutes the main area in which an often implicit sexism is perpetuated. This is done by reinforcing the woman's roles as the child carer, housekeeper and husband carer, whose primary task in life is to run a well-

organised and comfortable home. Complementing this is a tendency for social workers to treat husbands as breadwinners whose
main duty is to provide the means whereby the family can live.
Social work intervention then becomes limited primarily to helping
the relevant family members achieve these particular tasks. This
means that a breakdown in family relationships is seen either as a
failure of individuals to adhere to their allotted roles, or as the
failure of the partners to communicate their anxieties about their
capacity to meet the demands of these roles.'

(Dominelli and McLeod 1982:116)

In numerous other areas, social work practice can bolster the
family and the woman's role within it. Provision for the care of
children separated from their natural parents is one example; fostering and adoption into 'real' families, which is still seen as the best
substitute for the family of origin, is another. Children's homes and
boarding schools commonly use surrogate parental figures, 'house-
mothers' and 'housefathers', tending to carry out stereotypical gender
roles. Women workers do the cooking and perform the homely tasks.
Men are responsible for discipline, organizing games, and driving the
van.

The role of social workers in dealing with delinquency shows the
greater attention given by the state to the use of the family as a means
of discipline and control. Before the war, delinquent children were
generally removed to institutions. Now they much more commonly
come, together with their families, under the supervision of social
workers at home. The Ingleby Committee in 1960 emphasized the
need to improve parental performance and the 1969 Children and
Young Persons Act gave new powers to social workers to supervise the
families of young offenders. Ever since the nineteenth century, social
workers have aimed at improving the performance of working-class
mothers. In more recent years the Family Welfare Association has
promoted traditional feminine gender roles and tried to make
domestic work more efficient.

Modern family-orientated social work follows the lines of family
casework pioneered by private organizations and individuals on the
much broader scale made possible by the local authority social
services departments. It is striking how little the advent of the unitary
approach has altered the long-established traditions of social work

practice as far as women are concerned. Indeed, in every instance it simply confirms the drift of established social work practice. Even its more radical features, for example its promotion of community care as an advance on institutions, in reality means cajoling women into accepting even greater domestic burdens.

One of the central features of family life, and one sustained by the intervention of social workers, is the division it maintains between the private, personal world in the home and the public world beyond the immediate family circle. Questions arising from the personal and informal dimensions of patriarchal relations as part of a broader oppression of women have been a major area of feminist research in the last decade. The women's movement's insistence that personal oppression in the family and in sexual relationships is a political issue has challenged the idea that basic questions of women's oppression, such as rape, domestic violence, pornography, and prostitution, are private matters.

Sexual relationships are political because they are socially constructed within unequal power relations. For feminists, the very categories of masculine and feminine and the characteristics that conform to them are cultural and historical constructs. Similarly, violence and sexual abuse cannot be seen as questions of individual or family pathology – they are proof of male power in the personal sphere. Nor can women's control over their own bodies and their own fertility be reduced to a mere personal question. The demands for contraception and abortion challenge the public patriarchal alliance of men, church, doctors, and state to keep women in the role of breeders and sex objects in the home. Yet despite the fact that social workers are daily involved with the problems of domestic violence, abortion, and rape, most still operate with theories that are oblivious to the wide-ranging challenge from the women's movement to the notions of chastity, fidelity, and 'being sensible' that guide their interventions. For feminists, the problems that social workers are asked to deal with are not the outcome of pathological women or pathological families, but of inequalities of power in society.

The system and the state

All social workers in local authority departments, the probation service, and voluntary organizations work with other agencies of the

Welfare State. Some of these agencies, for example, the police, the prison service, and the education service, exercise considerable power over clients. Additionally, they may control resources that are crucial to the quality of clients' lives, such as housing and health care. Feminists have taken issue with the patriarchal nature of welfare agencies and the sexist values mediated through them. Social security, for example, does more than reinforce the economic dependence of women on men in the family. It encourages the use of women's labour at low wages while preserving the ideologies of domesticity and motherhood; the significance of the cohabitation rule as an explicit reinforcement of patriarchy within the social security system has been highlighted by many commentators. Lesser known, but equally significant, are the single-payment regulations that cover expenses incurred when claimants start work. These include a scheduled list of clothing and footwear which are considered necessities. This list almost totally comprises such items as donkey jackets, heavy industrial work boots, wellingtons, etc. There is no provision for buying a waitress's uniform, a set of office clothes, or protective clothing for cleaners and caterers. Is the assumption that women do not work? Or is it that if they do they must bear the costs themselves? Further examples of the workings of the social security system in relation to women are explored in chapter 3.

Public housing ensures that many women live in squalor while others are condemned to raise their children a hundred feet above the ground. It also privileges the nuclear family and discriminates against those whose life-styles challenge women's traditional role. Women who bring up children on their own and wish to live with other women in similar circumstances face this discrimination if they are dependent on the public rented sector for accommodation. There have been a number of women, with children, leaving refuges who do not wish to give up the support they have found in living with others. If two such women and their children make a successful application to a local authority for rehousing they are likely to be offered the standard accommodation for two adults with four or more children: living room, kitchen, bathroom, a 'master' bedroom, and two other bedrooms. This traditional response to the housing needs of the nuclear family is not adequate for households that do not fit the mould.

Apart from not providing decent and easily available treatment for expectant mothers, babies, young children, and old people (who include a large majority of the poorest and most ill-treated women in society), the health service plays its part in disseminating the ideology of women's oppression. Medical practice, which often incorporates social workers in psychiatry and general practice, proffers a particular definition of femininity. Doctors have been indicted for absorbing gender ideology into the definition of health and for supposing that women's reproductive capacities outweigh all other considerations.

Social work is welded into the regulation and managerialism of the state. Social workers emerged from a close relationship with state authority – as 'relieving officers', child care officers, probation officers, etc. – into a typically professional position from which they mediate state power and regulation in indirect ways. While social workers have statutory powers over their clients, and a certain discretion in controlling their access to financial and material benefits, their most important powers are more subtle. By negotiating the client's real needs with the availability of resources, social workers can press clients to conform to established patterns of provision. It is this reality that is suppressed in the notion of the social work task as the promotion of organic links between the individual and society. By conducting a relationship with a client on personal terms, the social worker exploits the client's willingness to consent to a degree of intimacy, while exploiting her (or his) personality to influence the client's behaviour. Every social worker knows the congruity of 'care' and 'control'. Care is one of the mechanisms through which control can operate – through the personal relations involved in social work and through apparently neutral means, such as the use of administrative criteria in decision making. This form of control is not always uniformly successful in practice. It produces its own resistances and tensions – defiance and resentment on the part of some clients and feelings of manipulating people on the part of some social workers.

The internal organization of the social work profession – its increasingly formal training and career structures – ensures some minimum of conformity of social workers to the requirements of the state. The bureaucratic and managerial character of social services departments operates to reinforce professional standards. The fact that the scrutiny and policing of subordinates by superiors is not always exercised should not disguise its existence.

Patterns of hierarchical control and supervision have been strengthened in the aftermath of the 1978–79 local authority social workers' strike. Professional qualifications are now mandatory for entry into social work practice and promotion depends upon the demonstration of good professional practice. Extra pay and additional responsibilities (usually the more delicate and coercive ones) are often only given to social workers after their performance has been closely monitored over a period of time. Yet the unitary method disguises questions of power and control, not only between social workers and clients, but also within the social work hierarchy.

Unitary method theorists have acknowledged the problems caused by the relationship of social work to the state, but they raise the problem only to dispose of the real issues: 'When a worker is at deadlock with a client system over an ethical issue, it is sometimes possible to shift the problem to a different basis or define it in such a way that other non-conflicting values can be brought to bear on the situation' (Pincus and Minahan 1977:50). Sometimes, however, the conflict between a client's interests and the demands of the state, mediated by the social worker, cannot be so easily shifted or re-defined. A working mother bringing up school-age children alone cannot afford to take much time off work. With the current levels of unemployment she can be quickly replaced, and dismissal because of unsatisfactory attendance is not a good reference with which to approach other employers. If such a woman wakes and finds that one of her children is ill, and relatives or friends cannot help out, she may decide that it is in her interests and those of her children to go to work and leave the child alone in the house. If a social worker is alerted to this situation through a call from a neighbour or the school she will be compelled to face this woman with failure to comply with the demands that the state makes of parents through child care legislation. The problem is defined as poor mothering, and the woman involved must demonstrate that she can improve her performance, if she is not to find herself involved in care proceedings. The problem of being a mother and breadwinner in a society that does not easily recognize and support that role is not at issue. The social worker involved will find it impossible to shift the definition of the problem away from 'poor mothering' because of the legal basis of her (or his) intervention.

The unitary method approves the power relations that prevail, both between social workers and clients, and within the profession itself. For those social workers who want to challenge their traditional role the unitary method is useless. Rather, it perpetuates those strategies adopted by social workers for dealing with tensions around their control functions, such as maintaining a distance from clients, sustaining stereotypes of clients, etc.

Pincus and Minahan (1977:92) attempt to get around the difficult ethical problem that social workers inevitably confront in practice by asserting some 'primary values' for social workers to follow. The first on their list is that 'society has an obligation to ensure that people have access to the resources, services, and opportunities they need to meet various life-tasks, alleviate distress, and realize their aspirations and values'. But social work primarily exists because society *cannot* guarantee people their basic requirements. Women have to try to realize their aspirations against their structural subordination and the burden of assumptions about their position in society, often visited upon them by social workers, among others.

The basic conflict between client and social worker arises out of the power that social workers have to decide key life-events for the client. As Pincus and Minahan (1977:93) acknowledge, social workers are potentially in a powerful position: 'Social work regards "self determination" as a client "right", but the worker is called upon to decide whether to "grant" this right to the client, and if so, to what extent. It is a contradiction for the worker to be put in this position. If the worker is able to deny the client's right of self-determination, then it really doesn't in fact exist.' This sums up the problem facing women. As clients their 'right to self determination' is ultimately decided by the social worker. Social work can thus be an incursion on women's rights, notwithstanding the professional rhetoric of caring and altruistic interventions to encourage 'self-determination'.

One example illustrates the conflict between the unitary approach and women's interests. Pincus and Minahan (1977:75) group police, together with schools, hospitals, and housing authorities, as a 'societal resource system'. But many women do not see the police as a 'resource system', but as coercive agents of an oppressive system. The police are unwilling to protect women against domestic violence because they respect the privacy of the family. In rape cases the police are notorious for putting the woman 'on trial' through heavy interrogation about her sexual activity. They encourage secondary control of women by urging them to stay at home at night. The double standard of the law fosters police harassment of prostitutes and leniency towards their clients. Again, real social conflicts are hidden behind a bland facade of harmony and balance. Social workers have to choose between activity as 'another societal resource system' – alongside the police, the judiciary, and the penal system – and defending their clients against state regulation and repression.

The unitary method perceives the state as a further extension of the individual and the community. The state is viewed as the representative of all individuals and communities in the nation, providing an arena within which conflicts can be worked out and change promoted. Unitary method theorists therefore enjoin social workers to become involved in pressing for social policy change through the normal procedures, as laid out in the appropriate systems diagram. However, they point out that 'society will not support any activity which has an objective of bringing about fundamental changes in the very fabric of social institutions' (Pincus and Minahan 1973:27). The unitary method theorists are pragmatic politicians: they counsel against anything more than reforms in the present system of society. They advise social workers to exert more pressure for the sort of administrative and legal changes that have always defined women as dependents and further promoted their traditional roles as wives and mothers.

In addition to confirming the power relations between social workers and their clients, the unitary approach serves a conservative function within the profession itself. It reinforces the stereotype of the traditional, female, caring social worker, although there is some recognition that the old construct may be in need of adaptation.

'The increased numbers of males that have entered the profession in recent years will certainly have a significant effect upon the choices made by practitioners since males are more likely to favour rational and instrumental behaviour and females the more nurturing and supportive type of interventions (although current movements for women's liberation may affect these differences).'

(Pincus and Minahan 1977:129)

The unitary approach does not confine itself to reinforcing the status quo for the 'client system' but also includes the 'change agent system'. The ideology of caring, or women's nurturing and supportive approach, traps female social workers into a traditional maternal role. Thus, the unitary approach reinforces reactionary stereotypes of the woman's place in every sphere of society from the nursery to the social services area office. The unitary model with its ideology of gender roles and patriarchy must be replaced. Feminist social workers need to develop an alternative radical model of social work, one that helps them rather than perpetuates their repression.

PART II ———————————

Women as clients

3
Motherhood

JANE CALVERT

Becoming a mother has a biological foundation. Pregnancy, birth, and lactation are all physiological processes experienced by mothers, and they can be very significant experiences. The intense love a mother feels for her child can have a profound impact on her whole existence.

> 'My children cause me the most exquisite suffering of which I have any experience. It is the suffering of ambivalence: the murderous alternation between bitter resentment and raw-edged nerves, and blissful gratification and tenderness. Sometimes I seem to myself, in my feelings towards these tiny guiltless beings, a monster of selfishness and intolerance. Their voices wear away my nerves, their constant needs, above all their need for simplicity and patience, fill me with despair at my own failures, despair too at my fate, which is to serve a function for which I was not fitted. And I am weak sometimes from held-in rage. There are times when I feel only death will free us from one another. . . . And yet at other times I am melted with the sense of their helpless and charming and quite unresistible beauty, their ability to go on loving and trusting – their staunchness and decency and unselfconsciousness. *I love them*. But it's in the enormity and inevitability, of this love that the suffering lies.' (Rich 1977:21)

While becoming a mother is undoubtedly a biological process motherhood as we understand it in this society is socially constructed. In other cultures mothers perform different roles, child care is not necessarily part of a mother's role (Mead 1935; Oakley 1972).

The expectations of motherhood reflect economic, political, and social changes. In our society motherhood is shaped by the demands of a capitalist, patriarchal society. Yet scant attention has been paid to this in social work literature. Professional texts and the discussions of motherhood on social work courses continue to emphasize its personal and psychological aspects. Based on ideas drawn from developmental psychology, assessment of the adequacy of individual mothers is still the dominant focus of concern (Riley 1983).

In this chapter I want to deconstruct the role of motherhood, to consider how our current notions about motherhood have come about, and to examine the ways in which the state contributes to the social construction of motherhood. In doing this I do not want to argue that there is a crude functional fit between the needs of patriarchy, the needs of capitalism, and the role of motherhood. The system of patriarchy was in operation long before the rise of capitalism. There are clearly two separate and not always compatible systems operating (Hartmann 1979). Motherhood is constrained by patriarchal and capitalist modes. At times the requirements of these two systems will be in conflict.

As social workers it is important to approach social problems not only with reference to short-term solutions but with the awareness of the broader social consequences of our actions. Social workers tend to work with mothers and their individual problems – mothers on supplementary benefit, single mothers, violent mothers, and depressed mothers. Each event is in its way unique and requires individual care and attention. But each mother herself is constrained by the social expectations and possibilities of motherhood. The only long-term way of helping mothers is by dealing with the larger issue of motherhood, and that requires an understanding of its construction and impact. Some of the crises faced by mothers cannot be resolved on a piecemeal basis, for many of the problems faced by women as mothers are engendered in the role expectations and social constraints of motherhood itself.

The construction of motherhood

Our current notions about motherhood were established in the nineteenth century. In pre- and early industrial Britain, a woman's major role was one of producing articles for sale, exchange, or immediate consumption (Hall 1982a). She produced children, but child care did not define her role or status. Indeed, children were not seen as requiring care in the way they are now. Rather they were seen as economic assets, as units of production. But as industrialization advanced, children's labour threatened the role status of male workers. The increasingly specialist skills required for the economy under capitalism meant that a prolonged period of training was desirable.

Prior to the nineteenth century, mothers were not seen as having an important role in their children's development. Child care, such as it was, was certainly women's work, but the same emphasis was not placed on it. Child care was not regarded as the fulfilment of a woman's life.

Until the nineteenth century a child with no father was referred to as 'the child of no-one' since the mother had no rights over the child at all. Only fatherhood was seen as significant. It was not until 1839 that the Custody of Infants Act provided the first formal and legal link between a mother and her children. It allowed the mother to have physical custody of her children until the age of seven, provided that she had not committed adultery. This was the first statutory recognition of the mother's nurturing role. It was after this that mothers gradually gained further rights over their children.

The rise of motherhood and the decline of fatherhood coincided with the changed status of childhood. Fathers had taken responsibility for children as economically active assets. But as children became units of consumption, they moved away from the mother's sphere of influence and jurisdiction.

Motherhood and childhood developed hand in hand during the nineteenth century. The education of children became a prime role of mothers and this of course was important in a capitalist economy that wanted to educate and train its work force. Developing at a time that Elizabeth Wilson describes as the peak of patriarchy (Wilson 1983a), motherhood also complemented the needs of the male work force to establish themselves as the main breadwinners and heads of households.

Social work was emerging during the period that motherhood was becoming an established social role. Given that children and mothers were only just finding their feet in their new found roles it is not surprising that many theories about how best to realize the fulfilment of these roles prevailed (Badinter 1981). The social workers were able to see a role for themselves in unravelling the problems thrown up by this new form of social relationship.

The processes of adequate mothering have been a central theme in social work theory and practice. But there has been a failure to recognize how recent such concerns are. Currently, we operate with a notion of motherhood as if it has always encompassed the same set of characteristics. Motherhood is seen as the natural female role; the ultimate in femininity. It is the world of men and male social roles that are seen as constructed socially and therefore appropriate subject matter for sociological study. 'Sociology is a science which has the whole social life of MAN as its sphere' (cited by Oakley 1980:71, from Bottomore 1962:97). How and why men engage in 'male' roles of economic production is well researched and documented. Motherhood, on the other hand, has been seen as a role falling outside the jurisdiction of sociological and social work theory enquiry. It has been accepted as a woman's biological destiny (Oakley 1981). It is only in the last decade that accounts of the social construction of motherhood have appeared. Motherhood continues to be discussed in terms of its relationship to other social issues, for example, juvenile crime, rather than with reference to its social constitution.

Motherhood is most typically dealt with in social work and socio-logical literature in terms of the relationship between child care and family break up. Here again, it is the naturalness of the motherhood role that is emphasized. Sally MacIntyre illustrates this well in her study of the medical management of miscarriage, where she discussed the attribution of normality and biological instinct to motherhood. This attribution is differentially applied by the medical staff accord-ing to the woman's marital status. Thus the married woman who has had a miscarriage is naturally assumed to grieve her lost child, as a result of her maternal instinct. The unmarried woman, however, is assumed to be relieved at the loss and is treated as a misfit if she does not display the anticipated behaviour. These responses are seen by the medical staff as biologically based (MacIntyre 1976).

Motherhood as dependence

Motherhood is seen as a vocation not least by social workers. It is a career in itself. Women feel that if they choose to become mothers or if that choice is thrust upon them – then they will not get involved in any other sort of gainful occupation. Motherhood is seen as women's economic role (Bland *et al.* 1978). It is this full-time devotion to the role of motherhood that creates many problems that women specifically face. Because no financial payment is made to all mothers (other than child benefit, which is merely a contribution to the expenses for the child, not to the mother herself), full-time motherhood renders women either financially dependent on men, or very poor, and most often both (Townsend 1979).

Women are expected to be both economically and emotionally dependent on men. The current British tax system illustrates this expectation of economic dependence very well. A married couple is classed as one taxable unit, and the man's wage is taken to be the basic one and the wife's income is added. Even though over 40 per cent of the labour force is female, and women make a vital contribution to the family wage, they are still viewed as economically dependent on men. Within the family the male is expected to be the breadwinner. Courtship patterns anticipate this stage of affairs, the female being taken out by the male. In marriage most women find themselves economically dependent on their husbands.

This dependence is carefully structured into the state benefit schemes. Until November 1983, married women, who constitute the majority of the mothers in this country, were unable to claim a number of benefits in their own right. Now women and men are treated as equals in certain parts of the state income maintenance scheme. Married and cohabiting women, who have recently been involved in paid work, can apply for supplementary benefit for their household, provided that they sign on for work. Women married to an unemployed man can claim family income supplement, provided that they are in paid work for thirty hours a week or more. This still means that the male is expected to be the breadwinner and if the woman works less than thirty hours (which many women do), she will be unable to claim this supplement, even if she is the sole breadwinner. This move towards greater independence for women could be viewed as an advance, a further inroad in the domain of patriarchy. However, these changes and their effects must be assessed in the longer term and in the context of a wider understanding of state benefits, and women's employment.

There is not a consistent theme running through these processes. Rather, there is clearly a high degree of conflict. On the one hand, women as a group are demanding equal rights and there is a good deal of liberal support for this. Some advances in the name of equality have been made on this basis. On the other hand, such advances have been made on a strictly nineteenth-century liberal model. Women are assumed to face state policies on an equal footing with men. There is no attempt to deal with the social and structural inequalities that construct a different role for males and females. There are now one or two instances where 'male' can be replaced by 'female' claimants. But overall, women are still presumed to undertake the domestic and child caring role. It must be acknowledged that some of the recent advances in the position of women have been made at a time when capital no longer requires a reserve labour force and wages are being held low. Such steps forward for women may not necessarily indicate that patriarchy is on the decline (Wilson 1983a), but rather that the relationship between capitalism and patriarchy is shifting and women's roles are changing as a consequence.

Such advances as there are must be seen in the context of the continued reinforcement of the patriarchal family structure. The invalidity care allowance clearly demonstrates this process. It is available to all men and to single, non-cohabitating women who have given up full-time paid work in order to look after a severely disabled person. The exclusion of married and cohabiting women from this entitlement is founded on two basic assumptions. Women are seen as dependent on a male breadwinner, their earnings being marginal, and married women are seen as the natural carers (Groves and Finch 1983).

Another example of the state's construction of women's domestic caring role is the ruling that requires mothers, and not fathers, to prove that they have made adequate child care arrangements before they are allowed to register as unemployed and available for work, and thereby able to claim associated benefits. This ruling, established in 1982, clearly constructs mothers as having the prime responsibility for child care, whatever the personal preferences or arrangements of the individuals involved. Such a ruling excludes mothers from the benefits of Manpower Services Commission schemes, such as Community Programme schemes, and from concessionary rates on many educational courses, both of which can offer valuable training for women. This exclusion reinforces the domestic and child care role.

Women are socialized into taking a dependent role and are seen as emotionally dependent and less stable than men. This view is held by those engaged in professional relationships with women, as well as by society in general. Answers to a questionnaire administered to a group of clinicians described healthy adult women as more emotional, more submissive, and less dependent than healthy adult men (Broverman *et al.* 1970).

The dependence, which as a society we have woven into the role of motherhood, is well illustrated by recent attempts to change the legislation relating to legitimacy. At present it is not considered sufficient for a child's welfare to have a mother only. A mother without a male for support is seen as a social problem (Holman 1976). Discussions about the problem of single-parent families assume a female parent. Proposals in the early 1980s to amend the legislation relating to legitimacy can only be interpreted as a means of establishing motherhood as dependent upon fatherhood. But the fatherhood that is being suggested is one that involves all the rights, but none of the duties, of that role. The proposals are intended to abolish the stigma of illegitimacy. In practice they would merely restrict the group to whom that stigma would apply. Legal measures already exist, to ensure that illegitimate children are not financially discriminated against. Fathers can also claim rights of custody, care, and access through the courts. The new proposals would establish automatic rights of fathers, irrespective of the mother's wishes or the father's social relationship with either the mother or the child. By this means, paternity, and thereby legitimacy, is extended to the majority of children.

The concept of dependence is bound up with the image of a woman as a consumer, rather than a producer. Although motherhood is thought of as a vitally important role, women in general, and mothers in particular, are not acknowledged as engaging in productive work. Motherhood is often seen as leisure rather than work. Looking after children is acknowledged neither as hard work, nor as worthwhile. The concept of motherhood as non-productive is integrally bound up with that of passivity and dependence (Mitchell 1971; Oakley 1972). The male's role as breadwinner and supporter is bound up with the concept of economic production. A man engages in work that is defined as productive, in exchange for wages that he then uses to support his family. Production depends on the creation of value, although, as Delphy (1980) has pointed out, value itself is a socially created concept. Decisions about how to accord values are made in the context of a particular social organization. The distinction between, for example, making bread at home or for the ABC company, is made on the grounds of social and power relationships, rather than the task in hand. Delphy concludes that the value of something depends on whether or not fiscal payment is made for it.

With industrialization, the production of goods that create value has become located outside the home. Productive work is linked to waged labour. This leaves various kinds of activity in a dubious and debatable category. A large proportion of waged labour comes under the category of service work, rather than strictly productive work. It does not create value itself but it facilitates that process. Art and creativity cannot be defined clearly in relation to the concept of value. Child care and domestic labour have also been distinguished from production. The domestic labour debate can be seen as an attempt to establish the role of domestic labour (including child care) *vis à vis* capital. It has been argued that domestic labour is reproductive. It reproduces the labour force, on a daily maintenance and sustenance basis, as well as on the more permanent level of human reproduction. Secondly, it reproduces the cultural relationship and values that provide the basic conditions of production (Barrett 1980; Bland *et al.* 1978).

Becoming a mother

The characteristics of motherhood as non-productive and dependent are precisely reflected in the process of becoming a mother, both physically and financially. Women who have worked in waged labour for a sufficient period of time and have paid the appropriate contributions are able to claim maternity benefit. The maternity grant currently amounts to twenty-five pounds (and there are discussions about its abolition). This compares unfavourably with other countries (see *Table 2*). Until 1982 maternity benefit in the UK was divided into two parts: the basic payment of twenty-two pounds and sixty-five pence and an earnings-related part. The disappearance of the earnings-related element has left mothers far more dependent on their male partners. Child benefit is paid directly to the mother, although either partner is entitled to cash the vouchers. It is,

Table 2   The level of maternity grants in Britain
and some other countries (1977)

	£
Austria	283
East Germany	279
Luxembourg	278
France	218
Czechoslovakia	106
Iceland	94
Norway	93
Hungary	72
West Germany	64
Portugal	29
United Kingdom	25
Australia	20
Cyprus	7.8

All prices are in pounds

Source: Oakley (1981:229).

however, a small amount (£6.85p in 1985) which does not cover the cost of a child's food, let alone contribute to the mother's expenses (Piachaud 1981).

Theoretically, it is no longer necessary for women to give up employment on having a child, and the Equal Opportunities Legislation and Equal Opportunities Commission uphold a woman's right to keep her job. However, recent work by Jean Gregory has demonstrated how ineffective the law is (Gregory 1982). Under the Employment Protection Act, maternity leave is an established right only for those women who have been in full employment in the same job for a period of two years. Since women's dependence on their husbands can lead them to move jobs to support their husband's career, many women will find they are overruled for consideration on these grounds. The nature of women's domestic role is such that they will be likely to take up part-time employment and to leave jobs frequently on domestic grounds (for example, family illness, school holidays). The Act specifically excludes small firms, which constitute a substantial proportion of employers of women. Consequently, many women will be unable to take advantage of maternity leave and will be obliged to give up work completely when having a child.

Women taking advantage of the current maternity leave allowance would be paid at nine-tenths of their pay for ten weeks, and half pay for eight weeks. They are eligible for a further twenty-nine weeks unpaid leave and their jobs are kept open until they return.

Britain might be defined as having anti-natalist policies. Hungary has developed an income maintenance policy, whereby a cash maternity allowance is paid, there is paid maternity leave for twenty weeks and a flat-rate child care allowance for a subsequent thirty-one months if the mother looks after the child herself. In Sweden the emphasis is on shorter hours for working parents of both sexes and full wage payments for either parent to stay at home for the first eight months of the child's life.

The social processes involved in birth also contribute to rendering women passive and dependent. The popular image of a new mother is of a soft focus photograph of the mother in a frilly nightdress with her hair arranged, not a drop of sweat to be seen, holding a perfect, already smiling infant. She is the consumer not the producer of the child. Frequently, the newly born infant is removed from the mother to be cleaned out and cleaned up before being wrapped in a sterile hospital blanket and handed to the mother as though as a gift from the hospital to her.

Modern obstetric techniques contribute to rendering women passive, dependent, and non-productive. Passivity is a construction of the obstetric team. Routine procedures reduce the mother's participation to a minimum. Women in childbirth have things done to them, rather than control their own actions and reactions. Medical contraptions restrict their movements. The popular dorsal position is designed for the attendant's convenience, and may reduce the efficiency of the delivery as well as the mother's ability to push and set her own pace (Brook 1976; Chalmers and Richards 1977). Passivity goes hand in hand with dependency. Since a fairly dramatic event is occurring, if the woman is passive then she is thrown into dependence on the attending staff (Brook 1976; Oakley 1980). She needs their help to relieve pain, to make her comfortable, tell her when to push, since she has been encouraged to mistrust her own judgement. Such processes are frequently undignified and unfulfilling for the mother. The lack of control may lead her to experience some form of depression or rejection of her role as a mother (Oakley 1980).

The historical events that have encouraged women giving birth to become medical patients have clearly contributed to the conception of female passivity. A patient is essentially someone to whom things are done. The whole ritual of becoming a patient makes women helpless. On admission to hospital her own individual identity is undermined by the exchange of her personal clothes for a calico hospital nightdress and the placing of a plastic coated identification tag on her wrist. She therefore becomes a unit of hospital administration for which the question of personal knowledge and desires becomes irrelevant. The woman is directed and instructed on what to do and when, rather than consulted as a reasonable adult. This process is not restricted to the birth itself but extended to both ante-natal and post-natal care.

This construction of childbirth as a passive event is not only a cultural phenomenon. It has been encouraged by the state. The state's involvement in the construction of motherhood as a passive, nurturing role can be seen by a study of state education for girls and its emphasis on housewifery and mothering skills (Ehrenreich and English 1979; Bland *et al.* 1978) as well as by the campaigns to get women back into the home and producing children after both World Wars. The state's involvement in the hospitalization of childbirth has had important consequences on the process of the medicalization of motherhood (Lewis 1980). It was only after the Boer war, when the quality and quantity of army recruits translated infant mortality into a question of the survival of the nation, that child and maternal welfare became a focal issue for the state. Although evidence existed to indicate that poverty was the prime cause of both maternal and infant mortality, economic solutions were not sought. During the nineteenth century, welfare policy was grounded in the concept of deterrence, and an attempt to maintain independence or dependence on a male breadwinner in the case of women. Furthermore, to have focused on the financial state of those women who suffered severely in childbirth or lost their babies would have been a dangerous strategy politically, as it continues to be. It is still the poorest women who run the greatest risk of producing a handicapped child or having a still birth. By structuring the problem as a medical one the state was able to establish some intervention and help without having a politically sensitive economic scandal on its hands. Medical issues were related to moral ones by showing the links between the spread of germs and lack of cleanliness (Ehrenreich and English 1979). Education of the mother on child care by the health visitor, for example, became as important as the question of how the birth occurred.

Ante-natal care became established as a medical issue in the early twentieth century, once it was realized that while infant mortality rates were improving, maternal mortality was on the increase. Again the issue became defined as a medical one. The role of the state and its involvement is of paramount importance when considering the prevailing ideology of motherhood. It is not sufficient to analyse the issue in terms of professional concerns alone. The establishment of certain medical professional imperatives was encouraged by the concerns of the state and the wider economic context. This process is not peculiar to childbirth. Indeed the medicalization of social issues is a long established means of depoliticizing areas of social concern (Szasz 1974).

Many nineteenth-century women's groups wanted to focus on poverty and economic issues. But the medical solutions that were presented were generally embraced, as they relieved the plight of many women whose lives were distressed at the experience of childbirth and child-bearing. Such acceptance was quite understandable and a woman's lot was possibly improved by these developments. Looking at these issues in conjunction with the development of obstetric practice clearly establishes the importance of the state's role in structuring the passive nature of childbirth.

The issue of passivity does not end in the delivery room, nor even on the discharge of the patient. It also forms part of our cultural heritage. We all learn something about birth during childhood. And what we learn influences our approach, not only to birth itself, but to all the players in the drama. To begin with, we rarely see a birth. Information therefore comes to us indirectly. It comes through books, films, and folklore and is therefore frequently caricatured and exaggerated. The essentials of the plot are right but the 'minor' roles tend to be played down and the 'heroes' to be over celebrated. It is the medical teams and not the mother who are seen as delivering the child (Graham 1977). As Newton and Newton observe in western cultures, the obstetrician says 'I delivered Mrs Jones' (Newton and Newton 1972:155).

The social lesson that is learned is more far-reaching than that doctors not mothers deliver babies. We also learn that the most feminine of experiences requires passivity. The lesson is that women need protection and referment to professional help in birth and motherhood. Since motherhood and femininity equal passivity, assertive, aggressive women who want to be creative and do things themselves are seen as unfeminine and unlikely to make adequate mothers. If we accept that motherhood and femininity are constructed socially then such medicalized childbirth must be seen as one of the major foundations of that construction. One of the essential characteristics of motherhood is depicted as passivity. Mothers cannot be expected to be assertive, taking control of their own lives, when the very process of becoming a mother is one that involves them in learning a patient role, accepting the expertise and decisions of others.

Motherhood and gainful employment

Motherhood is not only a cultural role and an ideological construction, it is also carefully etched out socially and economically. At a cultural level, women are expected to take full responsibility for child care. This comes about in part because of the concept of the 'family wage' (Land 1976; Barrett and McIntosh 1983). This concept has been the basis of male wage bargaining since the nineteenth century and has become part of an accepted tradition. Women's paid work is seen as marginal to the family budget, even though 40 per cent of the labour force is female and only 5 per cent of the population consists of traditional family units reliant solely on the male breadwinner (Coote and Campbell 1982).

But this image of woman as economically dependent is not merely a matter of culture. The harsh reality is that for most women combining motherhood with paid employment is complicated and exhausting. It entails dependence on others and finely timed arrangements for picking up and dropping off offspring. It can defeat women pretty quickly unless their income enables them to pay for these procedures to go ahead smoothly (and since women's incomes are 63 per cent of men's, this is rarely the case) or the family's financial position is desperate.

If mothers are to work full time, then typically their choice is to do what is known as the 'double shift'. If a woman is to do a job that starts at 9.00 a.m. and ends at 5.00 p.m. then her own working day begins much earlier and ends much later. Typically she will get up at 7.00 a.m. to feed and dress the children. This will be seen as her job, since her husband's role is that of breadwinner and he does not have the social skills necessary to do these jobs. She will get the children out of the house by 8.15 a.m. to be dropped off at a friend or child minder before setting off for work. Any lunch break will be spent shopping for the family. Arrangements will have to have been made for the children's lunches and for picking them up from school and minding them until the mother returns. After collecting the children she will return home at about 5.45 p.m. when she will feed the family and if she is lucky get the children ready for bed by 7.30 p.m. Next she will have to do the washing, ironing, and housework. She will probably have finished this by 10.00 p.m. and the rest of the time is her own. If any of these arrangements break down then she will have to go sick or get to work late. At work she is likely to be constantly tired and to be seen as unreliable. School holidays will of course present even further complications.

Many women who want to combine motherhood with paid work will opt for part-time work although it is often hard to come by and it does not provide the security, 'perks' or career development of full-time employment. For the woman who can get such work the problem of co-ordinating it with child care is not eradicated, only the balance has shifted slightly. She spends more time looking after the children herself, rather than paying someone else to do it, or relying on networks of family or friends.

Many women do want to be involved in paid work, despite the problems it presents for them as mothers. Audrey Hunt's survey of women's employment in Britain reported that a quarter of the mothers of under fives surveyed expressed a desire to work if child care facilities were available (HMSO 1968). A 1978 report showed that the number of women with pre-school children in employment has gradually increased despite the difficulties they face. This report found that out of the 900,000 children under five whose mothers worked outside the home only 12,000 were provided with local authority nursery places (Oakley 1981:230). Virtually no after-school care is provided despite the fact that an estimated two and a half million 5–10-year-olds have mothers in paid employment. Adequate provision for out of home child care is at a standstill at a time when the proportion of employed mothers is increasing.

There is evidence that being at home full time with small children without paid employment does contribute to depression in many women (Brown and Harris 1978). But culturally and socially we do not provide real opportunities for mothers to engage in paid work. Even though maternity leave is now an established right, many women find that they are unable to take advantage of it, either because they have not been employed with the same employer for a sufficient period of time or because their employer is exempt under the legislation. Even those women who do take advantage of this provision often find that colleagues are so hostile on their return to work that they are forced to hand in their notice for social reasons.

This assumption that mothers do not work is reflected in the lack of child care provisions both in places of work and through the local authority. This assumption that women will not take on paid work once they have crossed the threshold of maternity is engrained in all our assumptions, our thoughts, and our plans. While people have been busily thinking up ways of providing employment for school leavers, and the adult male population, the concept of 'full employment' itself simply does not include the millions of mothers who would like to find paid work. Of course, the issue is not merely one of finding a job, even one with flexible hours. The problems that mothers face are those of the domestic and child care responsibilities that are thrust almost entirely on their shoulders. Women not only need greater opportunities in the world of paid employment, they also need some relief on the home front.

While women take the lion's share of the domestic burden, finding or successfully keeping a job is exhausting (Badinter 1981:309). One of the key factors, therefore, is finding ways of helping men to achieve greater success in the domestic sphere, and thus to share that burden. And this can only be achieved if men are no longer seen as the main 'breadwinners'.

A shorter working week would allow more women to find jobs compatible with motherhood, and would also facilitate greater male participation in child care and domestic crafts.

Full-time, long-term involvement with small children can be rewarding but it can also become very tedious, repetitive, and emotionally draining. Child care of pre-school children takes place almost exclusively in the home and typically involves the limited interaction of one mother with one or possibly two children. This inevitably results in a limited range of stimulation for the child and isolation and frustration for the mother. Not only is this form of child care socially isolating, it also holds a low social status. Margaret Bone's study of 'Preschool children and their need for daycare' (Bone 1977) found that almost two-thirds of mothers of under fives would like to share the task of child-rearing with someone else. It is the production and consumption of material goods that holds a central role in late capitalist society. In order to locate children and child care more centrally, the whole structure of our social networks would need to change. But in the interim it is important to note that the problems women face in terms of isolation at home looking after small children, or the problems of lack of state provision of child care, are not personal, but social problems. They are the problems faced by a society that undervalues the production and care of children. Not only do children gain from the provision of alternative child care facilities, but mothers can be freed to engage in other activities, including paid employment, which will enrich their lives.

Conclusion

Patriarchy is not a static system but is in a constant state of change. Wilson claims that our society is in a state of transition from the height of patriarchal organization (Wilson 1983a). While this might be an over optimistic view it is certainly true that women have made certain gains. These have sometimes been as a result of a conflict of the interests of patriarchy and capitalism; sometimes the genuine victory of a campaigning group (Groves and Finch 1983), and sometimes Pyrrhic victories (Gregory 1979). But however such gains are viewed it must be acknowledged that patriarchy is a dynamic system. For every gain that appears to improve the position of women there are counter moves which take us a step further back. Currently there are suggestions of a right-wing backlash to the changing position of women in society (Fitzgerald 1983).

Social work with women tends to revolve around 'problem' areas so that interaction with women is likely to be based on a professional/ client model where the woman is being guided, helped or even 'cured' by the social worker.

'The "feminine" client of the social services waits patiently at

clinics, social security offices and housing departments, to be ministered to, sometimes by the paternal authority figure, doctor or civil servant, sometimes by the maternal yet firm model of femininity provided by nurse or social worker, in either case she goes away to do as she has been told – to take the pills, to love the baby.'
                                                               (Wilson 1977:7–8)

The development of this relationship of the professional administering help and advice to the recipient client tends to reinforce the cluster of attributes central to motherhood. The client is encouraged to be passive and dependent and to see herself as lacking in autonomy and authority. The casework approach can, therefore, reinforce the traditional role of mother. When working with families social workers often work through a problem in the context of the basic family relationships. The institution of the nuclear family and the roles embraced by it are not deemed appropriate areas for reflection, criticism, or intervention. In this way social work may frequently perpetuate mechanisms of control over women.

Judy Hale has argued, as a feminist social work practitioner, that feminist casework can change this pattern. She considers that:

'intervention with mothers should be used as a means to explore the reasons for their difficulties and to reinforce positive feelings about the strengths which they possess. An example of the possibility of setting the women's difficulties within the context of structural oppression is to acknowledge with the client the difficulties involved in rearing young children in isolation which, whether married or not, is the lot of the vast majority of mothers. Instead of an underlying paradigm of the intervention being an assumption that the nuclear family in its present form is an ideal to which everyone should aspire and to which most female clients are failing in their efforts to conform, the feminist social worker may have, as a basic premise, the view that women are struggling with an unnatural situation.'   (Hale 1983:171)

Social work with mothers should not only involve direct interventions where specific problems or crises occur. It should not only be about solving problems. The problems that mothers face are also structured by the social role of motherhood, by the social isolation, the emotional and economic dependence, and the lack of social identity bound up with that role. If social work with mothers is to be successful it means being aware of those issues at every level. It means fighting for the greater involvement of men in child care and for better job opportunities for women. Working towards such ends in a trade union or a local community group is as important as dealing sensitively with a crisis when it occurs. Where motherhood in particular is concerned, the 'appropriate' areas for social work intervention are those linked with the issue of material deprivation and its relationship to juvenile delinquency; or with the concept of the cycle of deprivation, child abuse, child guidance, illegitimacy and depression. Only in the last instance is the concern directly with the mother herself. In the others the focus is the impact an 'inadequate' mother might have on her family. In using this concept of inadequacy, judgements about good and bad, normal and deviant are constantly being made without any basic questioning of the social role of motherhood.

Where maternal deprivation, the cycle of deprivation, and child abuse are concerned, the adequacy of mothering is taken as the focal point and the more fundamental question of social organization, income distribution, economic and social policy are ignored (Holman 1976; Jordan 1974). Child guidance tends to focus on the adjustment and normality of the mother without any reference to alternative styles of child-rearing at all. Illegitimacy is treated both as a problem and as deviant, thus reinforcing the dominant view of mothers dependent on males. Even work with depressed mothers, although it focuses on the woman herself, is geared to encouraging her to 'readjust' to her family situation. The basic relationship between depression and isolated motherhood receives little attention.

It is important to treat women as intelligent, autonomous beings, capable of making their own decisions. Group work and community work may offer more potential than casework in that thereby it is possible to encourage women to set up and run their own groups. Of course, group work and community work are not necessarily more liberating than other, more traditional forms of social work. Groups can easily reproduce traditional role structures just as one-to-one work can sometimes create the appropriate support to give the 'client' the independence that can form the basis of social change. Where women are encouraged to set up groups, such groups may be able to campaign for changes in women's status by discussing issues such as wages for housework, child care facilities, and social security benefits.

Various accounts of such projects do exist and it is inappropriate to discuss them in detail here (Mayo 1977). Where social workers are called in to deal with a specific crisis, then group work has a limited value. In such situations it is attitude rather than the actual action taken which is controllable. Thus, it is important to engage women in debate about impending decisions and actions, rather than taking them without reference to expressed wishes.

Social work practice can only have an impact on motherhood if it acknowledges that motherhood is a social as well as a personal and biological phenomenon. It is by changing the way in which motherhood is structured socially that the lives of individual mothers can be improved, and this will involve political action, trade union and community action, as well as social work practice.

4

Women and mental health: towards an understanding

ANN DAVIS, SUE LLEWELYN, AND GLENYS PARRY

Social workers cannot avoid contact with the emotional distress of women. It is part of the fabric of their working lives and it takes a variety of forms.

At its most dramatic it plunges some social workers, approved under the 1983 Mental Health Act, into situations of crisis where they are required to decide whether a woman is behaving in a way that constitutes a 'danger to herself or others'. If a worker, together with a doctor, decides this is the case then compulsory hospital admission may result. Such procedures have consequences not only for the woman involved but also for others. Children may have to be received into care if there are no relatives or friends to look after them. Spouses and other adult dependants deprived of their main support, may require other services. If hospital admission does not seem to be the answer then the social worker may become involved in trying to mobilize scarce and insufficient community resources in order to resolve the crisis.

More typically, social workers in the probation service, voluntary organizations, and local authority departments find themselves confronted by the anxiety and depression of women trying to hold together the daily routine of their lives and the lives of their families, women treading a tightrope between coping and breakdown and consuming drugs prescribed by their GPs. Furthermore, it is often difficult for them (and for social workers) to separate out their individual problems and needs from those of the family of which they are part.

As 'Better Services for the Mentally Ill' points out, women have an estimated one in six life chance of entering a psychiatric hospital. The corresponding figure for men is one in nine (DHSS 1975). However, women who become clients of welfare agencies are at a much greater risk of hospital admission than this average suggests.

For a start, most women clients are, or have been, married. Marriage and its dissolution by divorce or death brings, for women, an increase in reported and measured psychiatric disturbance (Stein and Susser 1969; Chesler 1971; Gove 1978). Of those single women who have contact with social workers a substantial number will be caring alone for children or elderly relatives. Studies have shown clearly the isolation and exhaustion experienced by women in these situations. These are both factors that increase individual susceptibility to mental distress.

Highly relevant too, is the fact that most social work clients come from the working class, and the existence of higher rates of diagnosed psychiatric disorder among this group, compared to other classes, is well established (Dohrenwend 1975). Brown *et al.*'s comparison of a sample of women in an Inner London borough undergoing treatment for depression, with a random sample of women in the community, showed how much more vulnerable to depression working-class women with children are than their middle-class counterparts (Brown, Ni Bhrolchain, and Harris 1975; Brown and Harris 1978). Chronic financial and housing situations, responsibility for the problems of other family members, and isolation when children are young, are very much part of the working-class woman's world, and in combination can tip her from coping into a state of clinical depression.

Finally, as Groves and Finch discuss in chapter 5, many social work clients are elderly and the majority of elderly people are women. Ageing, which often brings with it poverty and isolation, increases the probability that mental confusion will become another problem experienced by elderly women clients, their relations and friends, and their social workers.

At any one time almost 60 per cent of the population of British psychiatric hospitals are women and 44 per cent of them have been in hospital for over five years (DHSS 1977). Most of them are diagnosed as having neurotic or depressive disorders, and an increasing proportion are labelled as elderly mentally infirm. Thousands remain in hospital not because they are receiving beneficial treatment but because there is nowhere else for them to live (MIND/Community Care 1976). The care that these women receive is determined by a variety of factors, which include their age and diagnosis, the predilections of their consultants, and the age and geographical position of the hospital. But entry to any psychiatric hospital is entry to a care system that has become known as the 'Cinderella' of the National Health Service.

Although 28 per cent of all National Health Service beds are for mentally ill people, it has been estimated that only 11.3 per cent of National Health revenue expenditure reaches them. A mere 9 per cent of medical staff and 20 per cent of nursing staff work with this group and as a result staff-patient ratios are far lower in this section of the Health Service than in general hospitals. There are also gross discrepancies in expenditure between acute hospitals on such items as food, laundry, and light. Many psychiatric hospitals are mouldering museums. Sixty-five per cent were built before 1891 and some are still overcrowded, despite the minimum standards set down in 1972. Within these general statistics there are large regional variations, some districts having hospital services well below the national average (Clare 1980; MIND 1982).

Social workers involved with women in this setting are working not only with personal suffering but also with grossly under-resourced care and treatment facilities. Physically inadequate and under-staffed wards increase staff tendencies to 'warehouse' patients, to fit them into routines and service them as objects not people. This process has been well documented over a century or more of asylum care (Connolly 1847; Lomax 1921; Goffman 1961). But until recently no consideration had been given to the distinct experiences that women have of institutionalization. Helen Evers' (1981) study of the differential ways in which nurses (mainly women) related to women and men patients on a geriatric hospital ward offers some interesting insights into this topic, as Finch and Groves discuss in chapter 5. There is obviously scope here for further work in relation to women in psychiatric hospital care.

Surviving as a patient is dependent on learning to relate and communicate with others who are more powerful in ways that might be inappropriate to survival outside. Regimes that develop on wards and in occupational areas of the hospital tend to reflect very definite notions of normality. Staff see indications of transition from illness to health in the adoption by patients of particular attitudes and behaviour and, as we discuss later in this chapter, there are distinct differences between what is interpreted as healthy for women and for men.

Staff views of what is acceptable and normal do not only influence a patient's opportunities within the hospital. Such views also influence professional decisions about resource allocation on discharge. For example, Ann Davis has suggested that many staff working in psychiatric rehabilitation programmes who are training patients for group home living in the community, hold the view that the firmest guarantee of a smoothly running establishment, giving little cause for concern to either the neighbours or the professionals involved, is a mixed-sex group home.

'Two men and two women are often cited as the ideal – because they "complement each other". The women settle into a domestic routine – cooking, cleaning, maintaining household standards – and the men engage in daytime occupations outside the home, but are available for heavy work, like gardening. This formula is often backed, where facilities are available, by additional resources directed at sustaining the balance. Day centre or hospital industrial-therapy places may be offered to the men of the household who find themselves unable to gain regular daytime occupation. The women, "naturally", find themselves occupied in the house.'

(Davis 1980)

Such decisions often have little connection with the choices that the women and men involved would want to make about their lives. Like much of the community care that is provided, it is reliant on the unpaid domestic labour of women.

The institutional responses that are currently made to women suffering from mental illness must distort the way in which social workers and others relate to women who become our clients. The very existence of a primarily warehousing service, which attracts so few resources, shapes the way in which we work together with our clients over mental-health problems.

The vast majority of women with psychiatric difficulties never reach the specialist services as either inpatients or outpatients. Shepherd and his colleagues estimated that in general practice, where the majority of psychiatric problems are dealt with, about twice as many female as male patients are diagnosed as having mental illness (Shepherd *et al.* 1966). Similarly, in Hare and Shaw's (1965) attempt to study mental health in an old housing district and in a new housing estate, women were found to have more psychiatric problems than men.

Questions need to be asked about the diagnostic process here. Are general practitioners and psychiatrists more likely to apply psychiatric labels to symptoms presented by women? Are women more likely to seek help with psychiatric problems than men? Whatever the dynamics of the process, there is little dispute about the general response of the medical profession to problems that are defined as psychiatric. The use of the prescription pad results in millions of women becoming dependent upon the products of a highly profitable drug industry. This industry has never been backward in its advertising. It demonstrates that what they offer can keep women coping with: child care; high-rise living; or the pressures of squeezing paid employment, unpaid domestic labour, and sleep into a twenty-four-hour day. Just as dropping into the role of psychiatric patient has its costs for women, so does the alternative. Coping, with help from medication, does not release the individual from the range of personal and family responsibilities, because she is not recognized as entering a sick role.

A browse through a decade of British social work journals (*Community Care*, *Social Work Today*, and the *British Journal of Social Work*) demonstrates vividly how little attention has been given to developing ideas that might inform social workers' understanding of women and mental health. Social work academics and social workers (who have committed their thoughts to paper) seem to have found it more relevant to focus attention on their own anxiety and depression about the status of social work among the psychiatric professions, than they have on the same conditions in their women patients. Pages have been written on the series of reorganizations that have hit the mental-health services, but the focus has been on the fate they have held in store for the professional social worker, rather than the consumer. Ideas have been developed that have justified an expansion of the social work role and the retention of specialist practice, on the uncontested assumption that more social workers in this field can only mean an improved service. The literature that has considered other mental-health issues has, in the main, avoided highlighting the condition of women. They are submerged in discussions of family therapy, rehabilitation, disturbed children, and drug treatments.

If one steps outside the narrow confines of social work and looks at the work which has emerged in feminist literature, one finds a range of ideas that are highly relevant to mental-health work with women. In the rest of this chapter we review some of these contributions and draw out the possibilities for social workers of an interactionist approach.

One of the principal reasons for a developing interest in women and mental health in the past decade is probably political, and linked to the growth and influence of feminism. It seems to us significant that statistics on mental health that have always been available are only now becoming noticed. Areas of research interest, like social work practice, are dependent upon their cultural context. The kind of individualist psychology to which social workers are usually exposed fails to provide adequate explanations of mental-health phenomena. Sociological research has much to offer us in understanding women and mental health. For example, a consistent finding in community studies of depression has been that women are approximately twice as vulnerable as men. The preponderance of depression in women is not just in absolute numbers of depressed patients, but in rates per population group adjusted for age (Weissman and Klerman 1977). It has been argued that these findings are an artifact or a response bias, where women are more willing to admit to emotional problems than men. Evidence concerning this is conflicting (Clancy and Gove 1974; Webb and Allen 1979). However, it seems unlikely that response bias alone could account for the clear epidemiological imbalance.

Psychologists and sociologists differ in their explanations of these findings, but we believe that no single approach deals adequately with the complex interaction of structural and psychical factors. Indeed, any simple formulation dissolves in the definitional confusion that plagues this field (Spence 1979). It has been noted in another context that definitional and methodological confusion often masks substantive issues (Levy 1981); we shall argue that such is the case here. The traditions underlying much work in this area have proved inadequate and this inadequacy is revealed in the proliferation of definitional, indeed conceptual dispute in the literature. There is a growing awareness of the need for new formulations that will be relevant to practice, and after outlining the existing traditions, we shall explore the usefulness of an interactionist model, while recognizing its limitations. Further work in this area, reaching somewhat similar conclusions, has been carried out recently by Warren and McEachren (1983).

The sociological contribution

We take the sociological approach as the one that examines the means by which social structures affect the individual. In the exploration of one of the most prevalent psychiatric disorders – depression – the research of the sociologist George Brown and his co-workers has had considerable impact (Brown and Harris 1978). They found that, if a number of predisposing factors are present, depression in women is highly likely to follow a serious life event, such as divorce, bereavement, or a child leaving home. The predisposing or vulnerability factors Brown established from *post hoc* analysis of his data were: having three or more children under fourteen living at home, being unemployed, losing one's mother in childhood, and lacking an intimate, confiding relationship. It is quite possible that in other surveys, further or different social factors would be found. The significance of these can be assessed from a sociological viewpoint without any reference to psychological variables, although Brown does suggest that 'chronically low self-esteem' could be a mediator. Despite the fact that it has been strongly criticized on a number of methodological points (Shapiro 1979; Tennant and Bebbington 1979), Brown's work has certainly been crucial in calling attention to the significance of events in the 'real world', and the environmental pressures to which women, and young mothers in particular, are uniquely subject. Both of these undoubtedly affect the prevalence of women from this environment as psychiatric casualties.

The everyday stresses of being a mother have also been pointed out by numerous sociologists who have studied the family, and the role of women in the family. For example, Gavron (1966) emphasized the difficulties traditionally experienced by women in both working-class and middle-class families, in that the needs of the individual women are subjugated to the needs of the family. The woman, therefore, has to obtain satisfaction vicariously through her husband and children. Yet in many cases these deprivations have now been exchanged for conflicts (Salwen 1975). Social and political changes have given some women considerably more status in relation to men than previously, and the number of roles that women can perform in society has increased. But housework and child-rearing are still seen as the primary responsibility of women, leading to doubt and guilt in the working mother, and dissatisfaction coupled with low self-regard in the mother who stays at home (Wilson 1979).

The concept of role has been important in approaching an understanding of the persistence of sex-typed ideology. For example, attention has been given to the ways in which sex roles are perpetuated through the family, schools, the media, and other institutions. The sex-role stereotype to which little girls have primary access includes passivity, dependence, masochism, and delicacy, all of which deny the individual's capacity to act decisively and purposefully. This may lead to a poverty of coping response strategies under stress (Block, Von der Lippe, and Block 1973).

The view of women as dependent may be stereotyped, but is nonetheless enshrined in our social structures. As Calvert discusses in chapter 3, the social security and tax systems work on the assumption that women are financially dependent upon men. The value of the sociological contribution is to draw our attention to such concrete social facts, and to point out that it is not legitimate to see the issue simply in individualist terms. Sex-role socialization is often posited as the mechanism for the perpetuation and internalization of sex-typed ideology. Yet sociological explanations remain profoundly unsatisfying because they fail to provide more than a superficial account of the prevalence and depth of the problems in most societies, and of the extent to which sex-typed attitudes and behaviour are so deeply rooted in most individuals. On the other hand, they do not explain how some women 'escape' sex-role socialization. In that many authors are themselves women, who, presumably, do not conform to the pattern, these theories are not reflexive.

The intrapsychic contribution

The second approach to women and mental health is the intrapsychic, or broadly, psychological. We feel that taken alone, this perspective is inadequate, but nevertheless has added a great deal to an understanding of women that is relevant to social work practice.

Bem, Spence, and others have investigated the psychological concomitants of sex-role stereotyping and have introduced the concept of
psychological androgyny. Bem has pointed out that the psychologically androgynous individual, one who possesses both stereotypically
male and female qualities, such as leadership *and* tenderness, is more
likely to behave adaptively than her sex-typed peers (Bem 1974).
Androgyny has been related to a wide range of psychological functions, such as creativity, mental adjustment, multiple personality
factors and positive self-attributions. It seems to be a useful concept
that respects individual psychological differences between men and
women, and highlights the psychological poverty of sex-typed
adaptations.

Within the psychological tradition, but on a behavioural level,
attempts have been made to describe the specific difficulties of women
that result from their 'reinforcement history'. The limited behavioural repertoire of women has been related by some to learnt
helplessness (Litman 1977). Thus, active coping responses are not
reinforced, so that women become in relative terms, helpless. From
this perspective a lack of assertiveness and other social skills have
been seen as individual problems, and treated by using techniques
based on behavioural formulations, such as assertiveness training
(Butler 1976).

Of course, one of the major contributions within the intrapsychic
approach is the psychoanalytic. Although by now it is almost
meaningless to speak of a unitary psychoanalytic theory, some
psychodynamic writers have characterized women as passive, narcissistic and masochistic. The healthy resolution of the little girl's
passage through the Oedipal phase has been seen as a renunciation of
hopes ever to obtain a penis and an acceptance of castration. These
views have been enormously influential and have been propounded
by a naïve disregard for their cultural context. Furthermore, they
have been interpreted concretely and used prescriptively. For example, Chesler quotes in *Women and Madness* (Chesler 1974) a number of
influential clinical thinkers as follows:

'But no-one can evade the fact that, in taking up a masculine
calling, studying and working in a man's way, woman is doing
something not wholly in agreement with, if not directly injurious to,
her feminine nature.'
(C. G. Jung)

'A personal motive will carry a woman through an almost un-limited amount of monotonous work, without risk of losing her soul. For instance . . . she can knit sweaters and socks indefinitely for her husband and boys . . . (woman's real goal is the) creation of the possibility of psychic, or psychological relation to men.'

(M. Esther Harding)

'I think that much of a young woman's identity is already defined in her kind of attractiveness and in the selectivity of her search for the man (or men) by whom she wishes to be sought.'   (Eric Erikson)

Although, as these excerpts suggest, many psychoanalytic writers have proved largely unhelpful to women, within this approach some feminists have found a perspective in which certain questions can perhaps find an answer.

'That Freud's account of women comes out pessimistic is not so much an index of his reactionary spirit as of the condition of women. The longevity of the oppression of women *must* be based on something more complicated than biological handicap and more durable than economic exploitation (although in different degrees all these may feature). It is illusory to see women as the pure who are purely put upon. The status of women is held in the heart and the head as well as in the home. . . . To think that this should not be so does not necessitate pretending it is already not so.'

(Mitchell 1974:362)

It then becomes important to understand why women collude in their own oppression. For straightforward economic reasons, it is easier for the status quo if women do see their primary role as dependants, but as Mitchell points out, this political explanation does not seem to be enough.

More recently, Chodorow (1978) and Dinnerstein (1978) have formulated psychoanalytic approaches to the psychology of women. The early experiences of the small girl in relationship with her mother is, therefore, not only crucial to psychological development, but also linked to social and political structures. Feminist psychothera-pists working at the London Women's Therapy Centre have devel-oped these ideas further. Eichenbaum and Orbach (1982, 1983) have described their adaptation of Object Relations theory for use in working with women. Concepts such as dependence and repression of the unwanted parts of the self, are central to their work, and much time is spent in trying to understand the significance of the mother–child relationship in the lives of their female clients.

An interactionist approach

It has become clear to us that explanations of women's vulnerability to neurotic disorders cannot be simply couched in terms such as 'sex-role socialization'. Nor do intrapsychic accounts recognize the importance of real patriarchal structures in the real world. Of course, it is not unusual for writers to assert that both social and psychological factors are important, but this usually implies that their effects are additive. This additive paradigm is itself limited and seems to be changing. At this stage it is at least an improvement to formulate an interactive model of women and mental health.

It seems to us that the system of gender is socially constructed upon its biological substrate, sexual difference. As such, it is a fundamental dimension in the symbolic order; the world of meaning that human language makes uniquely possible. This is why many feminists have been attracted in the past to the work of Jacques Lacan (Coward 1979). It is the 'taken-for-granted' nature of gender and its concomitants that makes the task of understanding the limits of its influence so difficult. As Einstein (1934) said, 'What does a fish know of the water it swims in?' Gender is perhaps the most basic dimension in the fabric of our social reality, and as such it structures the possibilities and alternatives for both women and men. There may well be surface manifestations of these constraints, such as, on the one hand, *traits* (for example dependency in women and hyperaggression in men) and on the other hand, *social structures* (for example, patterns of conjugal power or sex-typed occupations). Both are part of the socially constructed, and at the same time individually constructed world of symbolic meaning. As such, the arena, where the relationship between the self and the environment is constructed, becomes crucial. It has been argued (Procter and Parry 1978) that when psychologists recognize the inadequacy of individualist psychology, and thus leave purely intrapsychic formulations of mental health, they must come to terms with the social origin of personal constructs, and the dilemma of personal freedom in regard to a socially constrained environment. Therefore, an interactionist model of women and mental health focuses on the sense that the individual woman has made of her received social reality, and the price that adaptation to the reality has exacted.

The interactionist tradition in conventional psychology is in itself well known. Psychologists such as Mischel and Endler have developed person/situation models of personality. However, as Llewelyn and Kelly point out: 'to analyse social and psychological factors separately, implies that absolute and discrete categories of "social" and "psychological" actually exist independently of one another, even if they are seen as interacting' (Llewelyn and Kelly 1979). Indeed, we would wish to go beyond interactionism, away from the notion of the 'inner' and 'outer' worlds and transactions between them. Each of us inhabits only one world, and it is constructed using both social and intrapsychic evidence. Within general psychology, personal-construct theory is probably the framework most consistent with this formulation. (Although some work in this area was carried out in 1983 by Gore and Mangione.)

Such an approach would force us to examine aspects of personality that appear universally, but that have different significance according to the sex of the individual. Passivity is one such example. Friedman writes: 'The basic hypothesis . . . is that certain observed behavioural differences between men and women are the result of different degrees of societal permission for expression (acting out) of passivity which in itself is a universal longing' (Friedman 1975:408). We would argue that the meanings accorded to male and female passivity are different, are thus tolerated differently, and finally have different social consequences. For a woman to leave employment and have children is an acceptable way of avoiding conflicts with authority figures or with her own assertiveness. There is some evidence that male psychiatric casualties are treated sooner and for longer than females (Tudor, Tudor, and Gove 1977). This suggests that ensuring a man copes with his job is a very high priority among mental-health professionals. Equally, a traditional therapist is far more likely to allow a woman to escape from her responsibilities outside the home and to avoid dealing with her difficulties in asserting herself, whereas the man remains under pressure.

Implications for practice

Many social workers, on becoming aware of these issues, may notice their relevance for social work practice. They may argue that while it may be true that mental health in women can be influenced by social structures, when faced with the individual woman suffering from, say, depression or anxiety, such knowledge is of little use. Their task, they might argue, is to work with the woman in her social context, and they can no more transcend it than can the client herself. However, a failure on the part of the social worker to understand the implications of the socially constructed nature of gender poses serious threats to the female client.

The work of Broverman and her co-workers has demonstrated the degree to which the judgement of professionals is affected by socially held stereotypes regarding desirable feminine and masculine be-haviour. They asked three separate groups of clinicians to ascribe given characteristics to psychologically healthy men, women, and adults respectively. The results indicated that in many cases what was seen as characteristic of a healthy adult was different from what was considered characteristic of a healthy woman (Broverman *et al.* 1970). Kaplan (1983) has presented further evidence on the sexist assump-tions implicit in standard diagnostic practice. Chesler (1974) points out that, in America at least, the institution of therapy parallels the institution of marriage, in that the passive female becomes dependent on the active male for assistance, approval, and acceptance. This observation is consistent with Treacher's view that social control functions permeate the psychotherapeutic relationship (Treacher 1979). This becomes particularly important when the frequency of sexual relationships between therapist and patient in the US is noted (Holroyd and Brodsky 1977; Hall and Hare-Mustin 1983).

Social workers in the community and in psychiatric hospitals are repeatedly brought face to face with the way in which psychiatric institutions and professionals apply evaluative social and sexual standards to women. It is by no means rare, for example, for a psychiatrist or nurse to describe a female patient to colleagues primarily in terms of her appearance, to judge her progress by her feminine dress and make-up, and to evaluate the outcome of her treatment in terms of her adjustment to a traditionally acceptable female role.

An alternative approach is to resist the taken-for-granted nature of gender-related assumptions. In choosing this alternative, we acknowledge a tension between the universality of these assumptions in our culture, and their conceptual relativity. However, this tension promotes a keener appreciation of the social and psychological influences affecting women. This in turn leads to several important implications for social workers.

The simplest formulation would state that women are denied full adult status both socially and psychologically. Women are allowed or even encouraged to view themselves as dependent on dominant others, such as parents and husbands, rather than as autonomous adults. This dependence is reflected in concrete ways, such as the need for approval as a primary motivation. However, it is striking that in their roles as wives or mothers, women are also a source of emotional support and the regulators of expressive aspects of family relationships. In this way, women are seen both as emotionally dependent, child-like, clinging, and as having emotional reserves of strength and nurturant abilities.

We suggest that in work with female clients, certain issues recur regardless of the presenting problem. The issues are necessarily discussed briefly here, but have been developed further elsewhere (Llewelyn and Osborne 1983).

Need for approval, love, and nurturance

Research on achievement motivation has assumed that men are motivated by a need to succeed, and women by a need for approval (Sarason and Smith 1971). The notion of a fear of success in women is consistent with this. Competent women have been found to perform less well at tasks in mixed-sex settings than in single-sex ones (Horner 1972). This implies that success in competition with men carries with it the risk of male disapproval, that is, the possibility that competence is labelled as unfeminine. Despite the fact that further research (Spence and Helmreich 1972) casts doubt on whether men actually do disapprove of competent or masculine women, women's belief that they might, remains pervasive. We have found that the need for approval, to be loved by close ones and to be liked by everyone, is dominant in many of our female clients' lives.

There are two consequences of this. First, these women run the risk, through being nurturant and emotionally giving, of not having their own emotional needs met. In her search to be liked, by fulfilling the stereotype of the good wife and mother, the client may find she experiences a sense of deprivation of supplies of love from the outside world. She will often not be able to recognize this for what it is, even when the problem becomes acute. The client may experience instead a number of mystifying depressive or anxiety symptoms that may disappear remarkably quickly when her need for love, approval, and recognition can be faced, and felt. The woman may remain vulnerable, but can develop a capacity to tolerate her need, and learn ways of meeting it. Second, when the woman experiences hostile or angry feelings towards someone, these may represent a threat to her supplies of love or approval, and so may be unacceptable to her and will be denied. In this way she presents a 'false self' to the world. Awareness of her own negative or destructive impulses is split off, and the woman's personality is correspondingly impoverished.

For further exploration of women's needs for love and nurturance, and their roots in early life, see Baker Miller (1978) and Eichenbaum and Orbach (1982).

Low self-esteem

Related to a high need for love and approval from others are the chronic feelings of dissatisfaction with the self, which are often expressed by our female clients. This has numerous manifestations. First, there is often a large discrepancy between the woman's ideal self and how she sees herself. One common example is the woman's guilt at failing to meet her own ideals of motherhood. Second, many women seem unhappy about their physical appearance, having unrealistic images of the female body, and suffering persistent dissatisfaction that they are too fat, or too thin, or that they are repulsive or ugly. Sometimes this sense of negative bodily self-image can become so marked that it is in itself a major presenting symptom. Yet what is striking is the way in which such an awareness and dislike of one's own body is part of most women's experience, not just a pathological few. Some feminists (for example Orbach 1978; Chernin 1983) have explored the social and psychological meanings of the common preoccupation with weight, together with the diet/binge syndrome. They have related it to the conflicts facing the young woman regarding her sexuality and place in the world. Certainly, issues of responsibility and control, both of self and others, seem important in eating disorders. The autobiographical history of Sheila Macleod demonstrates this very clearly (Macleod 1981).

The third way in which low self-esteem can be manifest is in a low opinion of other women, who are seen as fickle, bitchy, unreliable, gossipy, and manipulative. Envy of successful or attractive women is also a common feature.

The view that a woman holds of herself can be changed radically by the experience of sitting down and talking seriously with other women. Thus both consciousness-raising groups and individual work with a female therapist can alter the client's view of herself. Kirsh quotes a woman describing the gains of a consciousness-raising group:

'I used to think that if I wanted to have a really good discussion with someone about ideas, I had to go to a man. And I now realize I turned that belief back on myself unconsciously and felt insecure about myself intellectually. In the process of coming to respect other women's minds, I came to have more respect for my own. Before this, I usually avoided doing things with groups of women – I guess I really bought the notion that things done with "just women" were somehow less worthwhile, less important and enjoyable.'   (Kirsh 1974:349–50)

We suggest that this is often borne out in social workers' experiences. A statement from a woman that she does not like other women is usually indicative of some profound, inner self-dislike.

Unfulfilled sexuality

Sexual problems are extremely common. Never or rarely experiencing orgasm is so common in our client populations as to be considered 'normal', although individual women vary in the extent to which they perceive this as a problem. The unawareness of how to meet their sexual needs mirrors the emotional dependence conflicts already noted.

Repeatedly, social workers and residential care staff find that girls at adolescence are not adequately informed about their bodies, and the first menstrual period is a time of confusion and shame. The majority of our female clients do not masturbate, and many have never masturbated. Some have a profound ignorance of their genital anatomy and the function of the clitoris. In a social climate where women's expectations of sexual fulfilment have been heightened by the publicity given to the existence of the female orgasm and female sexuality in general, the disappointment of these expectations can lead to frustration and bitterness. However, as women are viewed as responding to male sexuality rather than initiating sexual contact, even where the woman is aware of her sexual needs, she will find it difficult to meet these needs.

Sherfey (1972) argues that female sexuality is suppressed in our culture in order for it to be more easily controlled. Unrestrained female sexuality, she argues, would seriously threaten the male-dominated status quo. Since putting other people's needs first and maintaining a homeostasis in the expressive relationships in the family are two important themes for our female clients, it is easy to see why fulfilled adult female sexuality is incompatible with this. Certainly, within marriage there is much mutuality about the repression of sexuality. Hence, when the woman becomes more able to assert her sexuality, her husband is no longer protected by her denial, and may be confronted by his own sexual difficulties.

We are sure that these themes: the need for approval, low self-esteem, an unfulfilled sexuality appear frequently in the encounters between women clients and social workers. In some instances they are close to the surface, in others they are submerged in the presenting problems of women subject to economic and social deprivations. We present two case examples.

SALLY COX

Sally, a thirty-year-old mother of two small children, was referred by her GP to the social worker attached to the practice as a matter of urgency. When first seen she was in an extremely agitated state, and talked, in a rush, about intolerable and mysterious 'weird feelings' that made her, against her will, wish to jump out of the window or cut her wrists. The manner in which she described her symptoms was histrionic, almost as if she was performing a part. In her appearance she was extremely 'feminine'. The dramatic nature of her symptoms, and her gestures as she described them, were both seductive and unreal.

Over a course of individual sessions, the enormous, almost addictive craving she had for attention and affection became clear. Her self-esteem was badly damaged; indeed the problem came to be formulated in terms of her fragile and fragmented sense of self. She constantly saw herself through other's eyes, and had no underlying sense of what, beyond appearances, she really was. It emerged that as a child, following a damaged relationship with her mother, she had attempted to gain approval and recognition from her father by playing the role of provocatively pretty little girl. Her father appeared to enjoy and encourage this seductive behaviour, not recognizing the neediness it signalled. This continued into adulthood, when it came to be misread by men as a sexual signal. Inevitably, she came to feel profoundly misunderstood and abused, living in a perpetual state of *grudge* (Kahn 1975). Her hostility towards men could not be unproblematic for her however, as men were the suppliers of her narcissistic gratifications. Instead, she followed a pattern of 'punishing' one man by turning her attention to another. In fact, Sally had never experienced sexual arousal and fulfilment, despite her image of being a 'sexy lady'.

It is possible to see someone like Sally as the passive victim of sex-role socialization, as a sex-typed woman in need of assertion training. On the other hand, she could be characterized as a hysterical personality. We can also see that neither intrapsychic nor structural formulations give us an adequate grasp of the issues. An interactionist view might ask what sense she had made of her received reality, and what price adaptation to that reality has exacted. By the rules of our cultural gender game, one path, failing others, to recognition and approval, is to play the part of the sort of woman men are supposed to like. She had done this very well, and indeed she had been rewarded, in so far as she appeared to be a model wife and mother, and men *did* find her attractive. But the price she paid was exorbitant. And sadly, the inter-generational pattern was repeating itself. Her five-year-old daughter was a sexually precocious 'Daddy's girl', towards whom Sally felt envious and hostile. And yet, in her social context, the tragedy went unrecognized. Many people commented, on seeing Sally's daughter and her winsome ways, 'what a lovely little girl!' Sally, too, was a 'lovely little girl', but a lost and desperate human being. Her narcissistic needs were legitimate, but the ways in which, *given her familial and cultural context,* she had to attempt to meet them, proved disastrous.

CAROL EVANS

Carol, aged twenty-three, was referred by her GP to the social services duty officer for an urgent mental-health assessment. He said that she was deeply depressed and needed hospital treatment, but he could not persuade her to go. He asked for a section to be completed and her two children, aged six and four years, to be received into care because she had no relatives who were prepared to help her.

A visit by the duty social worker led to Carol's admission under Section 4 of the Mental Health Act 1983 to a psychiatric hospital twenty miles away from her council flat. The children went to a foster home. After two months of ECT and drug treatment a ward round decided that since Carol was taking an interest in her appearance again and was working well in the domestic rehabilitation unit, she was ready to return home. She returned and her children rejoined her. Six months later she was admitted to hospital again, following an unsuccessful attempt to take her own life.

Because of the social service department's concern about the future of her children, a hospital social worker met with Carol on a number of occasions. In these sessions the following emerged.

Carol married Tony when she was seventeen years of age. He was the first man with whom she had had sexual experience and her parents disapproved of him. She and Tony lived with his parents until she was pregnant with her second child, when they were offered a council flat. For the first few years of her marriage she worked hard to reconcile her parents and her husband, but they never got on. She ended up by going secretly to see her parents with the children, so as not to upset Tony who had told her she had to choose them or him.

A year after the birth of her second child, Tony began to stay away from home and he eventually left her to move in with another woman. Carol said she had tried to make a good home for him and keep him happy. She had tried not to 'nag' him about the other women and had never made demands on him about looking after the children. She felt she had 'let herself go' when she was busy with her babies and he had lost interest in her sexually. When her in-laws saw her after Tony had left, they told her that she had never given him the home he was used to. She had been too bound up with her children. Her own parents told her that Tony had always been worthless and she was better off without him. They asked her to move back with them, her father was retiring and they were moving to the seaside. After a lot of discussion Carol decided to stay in her flat and felt guilty about her decision. Her parents, she thought, had never forgiven her and she and the children only saw them at Christmas.

The year before her hospital admission Carol met Michael at a dance. They began to see each other once or twice a week. She found his company lifted her out of her life with the children and their sexual relationship was a revelation to her – 'I never knew that side of things could be so good'. From the occasional weekends he spent with her and the children she could tell that 'he wasn't keen on kids', but their time together made her feel good.

An anonymous letter from a neighbour to the DHSS about Michael resulted in a visit and an interview from a benefit officer. Her supplementary-benefit book was taken away on the grounds that she was cohabiting with Michael and he was working. She appealed against the decision and ten weeks later she appeared in front of a tribunal. By this time her rent was weeks overdue and her fuel bills unpaid. She felt unable to write to her parents about her difficulties because she felt they would tell her she had brought the situation upon herself. Michael lent her money for food but she did not want to ask him for too much.

Carol lost her appeal, the tribunal decided that she and Michael had a permanent relationship and therefore he should be keeping her. He moved in and Carol felt both resentful at his intrusion and guilty about the position she had put him in. He enjoyed pub life and she was grateful for what he gave her each week, but she could not depend on a regular amount from him. He left after three months, in which time their relationship had deteriorated. She claimed benefit again, but her debts had mounted and she felt hopeless and helpless about reorganizing her finances. When her electricity was disconnected she became very depressed and was compulsorily admitted to hospital a few weeks later.

She found her stay in hospital a respite from the pressures she had been living with and she was discharged as she was beginning to feel herself again. When her children returned from their foster home she found it difficult to re-establish their lives together. Money was tight as she paid off her debts gradually and tried to provide food and clothes. The children had been unsettled by the separation and compared their life unfavourably with the 'treats' they had had in their foster home. Carol felt isolated and lonely, and a failure as a mother.

In Carol we see somebody whose failure to be a successful wife and good daughter had left her with feelings of guilt and confusion. She chose, however, to continue to prove her worth as a mother. Her choice to remain independent of her own parents brought with it another kind of dependence. To support herself and her children she joined the millions of women who draw supplementary benefit in their own right on condition that they do not develop a sustained relationship with a man. When Carol became involved in such a relationship, one in which she was discovering for the first time something about her own sexual needs, she paid the price. The payment exacted was high in both emotional and financial terms and exacerbated her feelings of confusion and guilt about herself.

The response of both the health and social services to Carol's predicament was to return her as quickly as possible to her place as a mother without exploring in depth her feelings or offering her support.

When Carol returned home and was faced with her isolation and new problems in managing her children, her eroded self-esteem proved insufficient to sustain her.

Conclusion

In this chapter we have emphasized the very personal nature of women's experience, through mental distress, of social and political forces. That is to say, we have tried to explore the arena where the individual and the social meet and interact; the arena of personal meaning that the individual constructs. It is in this sense that we separate ourselves from an oversimplistic view of women as passive victims of a sexist society, while at the same time we recognize the all-pervasive nature of gender as a constraining force in our society.

Applying this essentially interactionist view in our work, our aim is to gain an understanding of how so many women never fully develop independence or adulthood, and how so many of our colleagues seem to collude, albeit unwittingly, in this sellout, accepting women's failure as success. This perspective places considerable demands on those who use it in their work with women. For example, we take seriously the fact that in legal and financial terms, women are dependents, but also the fact that many women have not the opportunity, wish, or ability to see themselves differently. At the least we should try to redress the balance in mental-health provision, which is currently stacked against women gaining full adult status, by calling attention to the very real factors that are holding women back. At best, we should aim to develop with our clients an awareness of the potential that they have to gain individual freedom within a socially constrained environment. We should encourage them to test out their new awareness in their behaviour, and to carve out, through their own experience, a different, more congenial reality. In doing this our hope is that they develop a sense of themselves as mature and competent adults. And, of course, all these things that we work with our female clients to achieve, we as women are striving to achieve for ourselves.

5

Old girl, old boy: gender divisions in social work with the elderly

JANET FINCH AND DULCIE GROVES

Introduction

Although elderly women outnumber elderly men as actual and potential users of social work services, most contemporary writing on social work with the elderly is gender blind. In 1979 among the very elderly in the United Kingdom (who, as will be seen, are much more likely to be users of social work services than the young elderly in their sixties and early seventies), there were twice as many women as men in the age group 75–84 and four times more women than men of 85 plus (HMSO 1982: Table 1.2). However, current British literature on social work ill serves those who seek to explore the significance for social work practice of this greater longevity among elderly women. There is little enough material to be found on elderly people and even less that relates specifically to elderly women.

One recent text, exceptionally, does pose the useful question: 'to what extent are many problems of the elderly (low income, subordinate status in society) the problems of *women*, irrespective of their age?' (Rowlings 1981:29). This question has provided a starting point for our own thinking about elderly people in a social work context. There are at least two senses in which specific features of the lives of elderly female clients reflect their biographies as *women* within the particular structural and cultural setting of British society in the present century.

First, the financial circumstances of the majority of elderly women are closely related to their marital status, in that the incomes of the current generation of women who have reached pensionable age (sixty) reflect, for the most part, the occupational status of current or former marriage partners. The retirement incomes of single women typically reflect a lifetime of lower-range earnings and restricted access to occupational pension benefits (Groves 1983). Second, the cultural image of what it means to be female and to be a particular type of female is extended into old age and then modified in ways that do not necessarily work to the advantage of elderly women. The prevailing images of women in western society have never been very positive (Stearns 1977). Thus, younger people may well conduct their dealings with the elderly on the basis of highly sexist assumptions about elderly women.

Evers (1981) has provided an account of this process in a geriatric hospital ward. She documents a particular range of imagery from which nurses derive a set of stereotypes and into which they fit elderly women patients and handle them accordingly. While we have not identified a similar study in a social work setting, it would be surprising if a similar process did not take place, especially in residential institutions. What assumptions do social workers, and others who deal with the elderly, make about appropriate or in-appropriate behaviour for women? How do such assumptions affect the transactions between social workers and their elderly clients?

Our main purpose in this chapter is to erase gender-blindness from discussions of social work and the elderly. In working through the implications of this exercise, we have become aware that it is imposs-ible to understand fully how sexism operates in this arena, without examining the extent to which sexism is itself affected by ageism. In addition, it is necessary to think through the ways in which both sexism and ageism operate, in the context of structural differences that are created between individuals on the basis of both marital status and of social class.

It is within this highly complicated scenario that we set out to offer some perspectives on gender divisions in social work with the elderly. That any attempt to define the 'elderly' by chronological age is problematic will be demonstrated in the next section. For our purposes we have classed people over sixty as 'elderly', since by this age most women in paid employment and some men have retired from or been forced out of such work (see OPCS 1979:97, Table 5.1).

We have tried to work through the implications of gender divisions in social work with the elderly by focusing upon three main areas.

What is the composition of the elderly population who form the potential clientele? What kinds of social work services do they get? How are the elderly portrayed and discussed in social work literature?

'The elderly' in reality: a genderless category?

The definition of ageing as a social problem is itself a social construction. As we have noted elsewhere (Finch and Groves 1980), the designation of an individual as elderly is also a social construction and one that is applied differentially to men and women. The latter tend to be socially defined as elderly a whole five years before their male contemporaries, since the age of eligibility for a state retirement pension is sixty for women and sixty-five for men (Thane 1978). Employers have replicated this by instituting a differential 'normal' retirement age, at which the great majority of women are required to retire from their jobs (Government Actuary 1981:40, Table 8.3). Sexism in official statistics (Oakley and Oakley 1979) is applied to the elderly in a rather unusual way. Men aged 60–4 are actually given honorary membership of the younger, 45–59 age group, and are thus excluded from the ranks of persons 60–74, which, needless to say, includes all women aged sixty plus (OPCS 1978:6, 8, Tables 1.4, 1.6). So men aged 60–4, typically still in paid employment, are treated as middle-aged. Women in the same age group, typically excluded from paid work, count as elderly.

Demographic evidence shows that the composition of the elderly population in terms of sex ratios and marital status differs markedly from younger age cohorts. Although there is a relatively small imbalance in numbers, as between the sexes, among persons in their sixties, at age 70–4 there are about one-and-a-half times as many women as men, and at seventy-five plus, two-and-a-half times as many women (OPCS 1980:2–3, Table 1.1). This imbalance increases more dramatically among those cohorts that have reached advanced old age (OPCS 1978:6, Table 1.4). Differences in marital status between men and women are apparent even among the younger elderly, and become more marked with advancing age: characteristically, an elderly man is married, but his female counterpart is not. Seventy-seven per cent of men between 70 and 74 are married and 60 per cent of those over the age of seventy-five. By contrast, 41 per cent of women are married in the 70–4 age group and only

19 per cent of those over seventy-five, an age group which, in consequence, contains a very high proportion of widows (OPCS 1980:2–3, Table 1.1).

An interesting demographic feature of the present generation of over-sixties in the considerable over-representation of single women in the seventy-five plus age band. Fourteen per cent of such elderly women are single, as compared with 9 per cent in the 60–4 age group. By contrast, divorced persons are comparatively rare among the over-sixties, though divorced women outnumber men by two to one (OPCS 1980: Table 1.1).

As for the future, very large increases are expected in the numbers of people surviving into advanced old age in Britain, so that by the end of the century there will be 20 per cent more people in the 75–84 age band and 58 per cent more in the 85 plus group (OPCS 1978:8, Table 1.6). Barring some dramatic change in the life-expectancy pattern of the sexes, most of these survivors will be women.

The picture that we have sketched briefly, demonstrates the importance of gender differences among the population of elderly with which social workers potentially do, and will, have dealings. Such dealings are usually concerned with both basic living arrangements and the financial circumstances of the elderly. Again, gender divisions are of considerable importance. As we have indicated elsewhere (Finch and Groves 1980) elderly men usually reside with, and/or are cared for by, close kin – typically females – while large numbers of elderly women live alone and the number of such one-person households is increasing. The likelihood of living in a residential institution increases markedly after the age of seventy-five and, since more women are likely to survive to an advanced age, there is a preponderance of women in old people's accommodation (Hunt 1978:41). Moreover, among the very elderly, the never-married are 'high risk' when it comes to the likelihood of being in an institution in old age, though family status (and especially the presence or absence of children) is only slightly less crucial (Townsend 1981:15). Thus the basic living arrangements of elderly men and elderly women are often rather different, with women more likely than men either to be living alone or in residential care.

Gender is an equally important feature of variations in the financial circumstances of the elderly, cross-cut by social-class variations, as measured by former occupational status. Again, the greater

likelihood that women will survive into extreme old age is important. Elderly women (and the non-married in particular) are over-
represented among the very poor. Income levels decline with age
(Hunt 1978:5). The current generation of elderly people, and especially the women, have had restricted access to the benefits of
occupational pension schemes. Few women have earned such benefits
in their own right – a reflection of their low-paid, part-time and
interrupted employment histories (Walker 1981:87) and their exclusion from such schemes (Groves 1983). The proportion of widows in
receipt of occupational widow's pensions declines steeply with age.
Among the most elderly, a minority of husbands had access to
occupational pensions and fewer still were in schemes that provided
widows' pensions (Groves 1983).

For women in particular, financial circumstances in old age are
related not only to their previous employment history, but, crucially,
also to their former marital status, a factor that is virtually irrelevant
for men. Townsend's survey of a group of over sixty-fives in 1969,
found a clear association between poverty and 'non-married status'.
Four-fifths of this group, composed largely of women, were living at or
near supplementary benefit rate. He commented:

'Through the institution of marriage, women are both deprived of
male privileges to certain individual rights to income, and entitled
to a share of the financial prerogatives of men. After reaching the
pensionable age, some married women are cushioned from falling
into poverty. Those whose husbands have already died or become
separated from them, or whose husbands subsequently do so, are
exposed to greater risks of both social isolation and financial loss.'
(Townsend 1979:811)

While emphasizing that old age is not of itself problematic, in this
section we have tried to draw attention to the more problematic issues
that affect some (but not all) of the elderly, especially the very elderly.
Our main purpose, however, has been to demonstrate that the
treatment of the 'elderly' as a genderless category obscures not only
the fact that the majority of the elderly (especially the very elderly) are
women, but also that the prospects for one's lifestyle in old age are
very different for men and for women, and different between women
according to marital status. In so far as social workers themselves

follow this cultural practice of treating 'the elderly' as a gender-less category, they inevitably work with a distorted view of a group that forms a significant part of their actual and potential clientele.

Social work services and elderly people

Elderly people do form quite a large proportion of the individuals with whom social work services have contact. The main initial point of contact appears to be with local authority social service departments, though voluntary agencies are also active in this field. How are their needs perceived and handled? What kinds of services do they receive? Who delivers those services? While it is beyond the scope of this chapter to consider those issues fully in general terms, they will be considered here in relation to the ways in which gender divisions actually appear to operate in the delivery of social work services to the elderly.

The main theme of this section is that while social workers, along with most other people, may be gender-blind in their explicit thinking about the elderly, they still can (and it appears, often do) operate with implicit gender assumptions in their dealings with elderly clients. These assumptions seem to operate on at least three levels, which are treated separately here, although clearly they are interlinked: the ways in which elderly people come to be defined as clients of social services departments; the kinds of services regarded as suitable for them; and arrangements for their 'care'.

BECOMING AN ELDERLY CLIENT

The process of becoming a client of the social services department seems to vary markedly for the younger and older elderly. On the evidence of the Southampton study of a local social services department, many 'referrals' in the 64–75 age group are self-referrals, involving equal numbers of men and women. By contrast, the over 75s were usually referred by a third party, often the health services, and mainly because of infirmity and physical disability. Self-referrals were rare in the 75 plus age group (Goldberg *et al.* 1977). These third-party referrals characteristic of older clients were often based on an assessment (not made by the client him or herself) that physical health and/or domestic circumstances had reached a point that required some kind of social services department intervention. Often this was said to be the result of the inability of someone else in the household to provide care and to reflect 'the mounting burden upon relatives who were themselves ageing' (Goldberg *et al.* 1977:264).

It seems likely, therefore, that the designation of an elderly person's circumstances as warranting social work intervention are partly dictated by cultural norms about what family, friends, and neighbours find acceptable and tolerable, which may itself be linked to the sex of the elderly person. This applies with special force to the elderly who are mentally ill, many of whom are women. Jefferys has noted that women of sixty-five and over occupy an average 62 per cent of all beds for female patients in psychiatric hospitals, while men of the same age occupy only 39 per cent of male beds (Jefferys 1977:15). While part of this discrepancy is presumably explained by differential rates of survival into old age, Jefferys argues that:

> 'It would seem that mental illness, when it occurs, takes a more serious form among the elderly and especially among women, than it does among younger age groups or that, when it occurs among the elderly, it is more difficult for others to tolerate in a community setting.'   (Jefferys 1977: 15)

It seems reasonable to speculate further that certain types of social behaviour (whether or not they are linked as symptoms of mental illness), which are regarded as tolerable in younger people, may be regarded as signs that some sort of social intervention is called for in the case of the elderly. In this context it is interesting to consider so-called aggressive behaviour. To what extent may an elderly woman be labelled as aggressive (and maybe by implication abnormal) by her GP or social worker, when her assertive behaviour would be tolerated in an elderly man and probably viewed as normal in a young man? This is the kind of issue to which any social work practice that is not gender-blind should be sensitive. As Evers' (1981) account of a geriatric hospital ward demonstrates, 'The women patients tend to be subjected to particular strategies of insidious oppression: the nurses – also women on the whole – tend to label women patients as stereotypically more "difficult" than men'.

Equally, it seems likely that assessments of an elderly person's capacity to carry out certain tasks in the home, so often part of a decision about their need for social work intervention (Townsend 1981:17), commonly incorporates gender stereotypes. It can apply to assessments related to provision of home-helps, access to residential care, and to presumed ability to look after, say, a disabled elderly spouse. Hunt's study of elderly people living at home listed the percentages of over 65s, by sex, who were unable to perform certain domestic tasks. Nearly a quarter of the men (all ages) were apparently unable to do 'little sewing jobs', and 35 per cent of even the youngest group of women (65–9) were unable to do, 'minor repairs, e.g. fuses'. Of course, both these tasks require reasonable eyesight and a degree of manual dexterity, but Hunt comments aptly that, 'it seems likely that many of the differences between men and women's abilities are more a product of ignorance than of physical differences' (Hunt 1978:8).

The recognition of gender stereotyping in presumed ability to perform certain domestic tasks raises the important issue of whether, in effect, elderly men and women have differential access to services, by being assessed on the basis of such stereotypes. Is an elderly man, for example, more likely to be allocated a home-help than an elderly woman of equal physical incapacity, precisely because, as a man, he is presumed to be more in need of domestic assistance? In so far as social workers, along with doctors, act as important gatekeepers to services for elderly people, there is the possibility that their decisions effectively reinforce the operation of gender divisions. Indeed, without explicit attempts to counteract that, it seems likely that this *will* happen, since the processes through which clients come to the attention of the social services department tend themselves to be imbued with gender-based assumptions.

RECEIVING A SERVICE

What kinds of services are elderly clients thought to be in need of? What kinds of services do they actually receive? And, in particular, do elderly people get *social work* services from social services departments?

The evidence from the Southampton study of a year's intake into a social services area office is that in the main the elderly receive practical help and advice and appear to be among the most satisfied clients (Goldberg 1979:4). Most of the contact was short term and resulted in practical provision, such as allocation of a home-help. The evidence was that most elderly people with whom the social service departments came into contact did not become part of long-term caseloads: when they did, the object appeared to be a form of surveillance. The aim of the social workers in most cases was to preserve the status quo – in only one-fifth of the cases was there any aim of improving the life or greater well-being of elderly clients (Goldberg *et al*. 1978).

The emphasis upon practical help to the exclusion of other types of help has been criticized by Rowlings (Rowlings 1981:56) and by Brearley:

> 'Social work provision for ageing clients has too often been based on a stereotyped view – old people need only practical services – the unspoken addition is that the success of social work in this view is the death of the client who can then be removed from the caseload.'
> (Brearley 1975:108)

Why is it that so little social work with the elderly seems to involve activities traditionally central to social work, especially short-term casework, designed to bring about changes in the client's situation and/or her ability to handle it? Failure to engage in casework with elderly clients primarily is attributed by writers on the subject both to the belief that it would not be effective and to the inherent difficulties for any social worker who undertakes it. The capacity of the elderly client for growth and change appears to be in doubt, although this view has been challenged recently (Brearley 1978:183; Holloway 1980). Even the BASW guidelines on social work with the elderly (BASW 1977) de-emphasize casework. These envisage that the type of work undertaken by a trained social worker should often include arranging for services to be provided by unqualified people and mobilizing community care (points to which we shall return). A more recent BASW discussion document does envisage the need for the involvement of professionally trained social workers in casework with the elderly (BASW 1982) but there is no indication as to how this could be achieved within existing resources and given alternative emphasis in public policy.

If casework with the elderly is little practised, group work, which Brearley regards as potentially useful, appears to be even less developed, although there are one or two examples of it (Cooper 1980).

Brearley warns that old people may fear that they cannot see or hear well enough to participate in a group and that due to 'poor self-image' they may find it difficult to participate (Brearley 1975:79). Similarly, community work with the elderly seems to be very under explored. While it is the unusual social service department that fosters client community action of a political nature, community self-help of a somewhat sex-stereotyped nature is reflected in the literature. One account of encouraging community groups of the elderly on housing estates featured tea parties involving old ladies disinterring their best tablecloths (Brearley 1974). Discussions of community work in a social work setting often move little beyond notions of community care and self-help which, at best, may involve co-opting the young elderly into volunteer work.

To sum up, the elderly appear to derive such social work services as they get mainly from social service departments in the form of short term and/or practical help, or longer-term surveillance. Little case-work and even less group and community work is available, the rationale for which seems to be the highly ageist assumption that elderly people cannot benefit from the most high-status services that social workers provide.

A further dimension to this is revealed by looking at the question of who actually provides the services that the elderly do receive. Then it immediately becomes apparent that not only is work with the elderly low-status work, but it is mostly carried out by low-status workers (Brearley 1978:172; Rowlings 1981:17). There appears to be ample evidence that elderly clients are usually assigned to social work assistants (Holme and Maizels 1978; Stevenson and Parsloe 1978). In the Southampton study, qualified social workers were involved in 69 per cent of elderly client cases, but most of these were carried out on a day-to-day basis by two former welfare officers who had a special interest in the elderly: none of the recently qualified social workers had more than one or two 'elderly' cases, apart from the senior (Goldberg et al. 1978:259).

Although many authorities now have a high percentage of qualified staff, it is functional for them to provide social work assistants for cost-saving reasons. A social work assistant is normally a non-career grade, and thus, not surprisingly, a grade that appears to be over-whelmingly the prerogative of women. In 1976 there were 2,522 social work assistants employed in England and Wales, of whom 83 per cent were female (Popplestone 1980). It should also be noted that the vast majority of residential care assistants and home-helps – the other main groups of social service department employees who have close contact with the elderly – are women.

Thus, the elderly as social work clients appear to receive a limited range of low-status services, delivered by low-status workers. The ageist assumption that they need low-status services only is reinforced by the allocation of low-status workers to them, which itself can be seen as ageist (Age Concern 1981:11–12). This itself is a matter for concern, and doubly so, precisely because the likelihood that an elderly client is in practice a woman increases with advancing age. Indeed, the whole process is effectively women only: low-status services delivered to elderly women by low-status women workers of a younger generation.

BEING CARED FOR

One of the major points at which social services departments become involved with an elderly person is when she or he becomes sufficiently incapacitated to need fairly constant personal care. On an individual level, this involves assessments of the person's needs and decisions about access to services. At an institutional level, it involves social services departments in the provision of residential care, and increasingly in the development of community-based alternatives. A consideration of social services' involvement in decisions and plans about the provision of care, raises, from the point of view of gender divisions, important questions not only about those who receive the service, but also about those who provide it.

The idea that residential care for the elderly should be provided as a last resort only is strongly entrenched in the literature both of social work and of social policy, although, as we have argued elsewhere (Finch and Groves 1981), there are good grounds for challenging this view from a feminist perspective. Some writers have argued that the case for community care has been overstated, on the grounds that residential care should not be seen merely as a last resort, or that it is not necessarily more expensive than a heavy input of domiciliary services (Armitage 1979). Arie provides a powerful argument against non-residential care for the demented on the grounds that people suffering from dementia can never be left totally unsupervised and that: 'Such round-the-clock care in the home is one thing that can never be provided by the statutory services; institutions exist precisely because they are the only economic way of providing this care for large numbers of people' (Arie 1977:77).

Such enthusiasm for residential care is, however, a minority taste at the present time, in comparison with the powerful lobby spearheaded by the Conservative Government, which favours the expansion of community care. Care 'by' the community, mobilizing volunteer and unpaid domestic labour, is the preferred version of community care (Finch and Groves 1980). In organizational terms there are two versions of care by the community currently being publicized as models for cost-effective social service department practice: 'patch-based' social work and what might be termed 'intensive' community care. Both of these scenarios designate the professional social worker as the key figure who orchestrates the delivery of domiciliary care services to those most frail and dependent members of the community who would otherwise be candidates for some sort of institutional care.

Under the patch-based system (Cooper *et al.* 1975; Hadley and McGrath 1980) teams of social work assistants, paid volunteers, and unpaid carers operate in small geographical areas under the supervision of a professional social worker who interweaves social work and the community. The system appears to involve an upwardly mobile and career-oriented male patch-leader (Hadley and McGrath 1980:35) with a train of female patchworkers (alias social work assistants), home-helps, and wardens (Hadley 1981:43). The highly sexist expectations of the kinds of people who will be available for this work are very clear in the sketch given by Cooper *et al.* of the typical 'warden' in the patchwork scheme that they envisage: 'Usually middle-aged and married, with some experience of life . . . it is unlikely that she will move, or have particular ambitions, and therefore provides a continuity with her clients' (Cooper *et al.* 1975:9).

The 'intensive' community care system has been pioneered by Kent social services in collaboration with the University of Kent and involves oversight by a professional social worker with a budget for 'buying in' domiciliary help. The total budget allowed is much less than the cost of residential care and a key purchase is the service of low-paid volunteers who provide intensive service. Advocates of this scheme have a remarkable way of conceptualizing their plans, which they call 'advancing the technology of domestic support' (Kent Community Care Project 1979:21).

If these kind of schemes become increasingly popular, the care of the frail elderly in the future will be handled mainly through the offices of low-paid workers and paid volunteers, most of them women, with the front-line caring carried out almost exclusively by female relatives (Finch and Groves 1983). The implications of this are little discussed in the literature that enthusiastically promotes community care and envisages social workers as mobilizers of community resources.

The Barclay Report on the role and task of social workers (NISW 1982) advocates a form of 'community social work' that would mobilize informal caring networks and operate in partnership with them. At no point does the Barclay Report address itself to issues of gender in relation to paid workers, volunteers, or carers. Evidence that carers are women is treated as an unproblematic fact (NISW 1982:75, 200). While it is argued that such care is sometimes given 'at great personal cost', which might be alleviated by an input of community social work, no basic questions are asked about the concept of informal care by women. Indeed, the working party appears to have had an extremely sex-stereotyped view of the roles of adult children in the informal care of the elderly, depicting 'an elderly person in Haringey' with 'a son in Brighton who sees to her finances, a daughter in Enfield who comes over twice a week to do a bit of cleaning and who always brings a casserole with her' (NISW 1982:205–06).

The chances that these issues of gender division will be recognized within social services departments as they attempt to mobilize voluntary resources, are not increased by the distribution of men and women staff in social services hierarchies. Popplestone, in her study of the under-representation of women in senior-management posts in the social services departments, argues that social work is a profession that, in its basic grades, provides opportunities for women to use 'the caring and nurturing qualities which are culturally assigned to women in this society'. It is very pertinent to ask how far traditional attitudes towards the roles of the sexes are reflected in the practice of the (predominantly female) basic and senior 'professional' social workers and the (predominantly male) senior management. In the absence of systematic evidence, one can only speculate that there is unlikely to be widespread radical variation from the norms of the culture in which social services operate (Popplestone 1980).

These issues of gender are important at an institutional level and in the planning of social service provision, but they are also reflected at an individual level, when decisions are taken about how care should be provided and by whom. As we have already argued, social workers can and do operate with particular notions of gender when they act as gatekeepers to services, and these can apply as much to potential carers as to the elderly themselves.

There is evidence that the kind of service that an elderly person living in his or her own home is likely to receive is closely related to their marital and kinship status. Those with no surviving spouse or children are most likely to receive assistance in the absence of approved, culturally designated carers. Townsend notes that 44 per cent of single women and 37 per cent of single men over ninety were in residential care as of the Census of 1971 (Townsend 1981:17).

That the care of the dependent elderly by the community depends so fundamentally on the family circumstances of the caring person and the continuing willingness of female relatives to take on the burden of care inevitably raises the question: to what extent are social workers, in their role as gatekeepers and guardians of scarce resources, active in perpetuating inequalities based on family status and reinforcing women in their designated natural caring roles? Reliance on caring relatives is, on the face of it, an easy solution: it is to be hoped that more will become known about the costs of this mode of care provision in terms of the effects on the physical and mental health of carers. As Brearley remarks, 'integration and independence are not desirable objectives if they place an unbearable burden on a daughter' (Brearley 1978:189).

As Rowlings argues in relation to whether former carers should be expected to take back an elderly person ready for discharge from hospital, 'The social worker may be in a position of considerable influence over discharge arrangements and the amount of persuasion which should be exerted' (Rowlings 1981:101). It is encouraging, therefore, that a recent BASW document recognizes that it is all too easy to assume that a woman relative will take care of an elderly dependant, stating unequivocally that, 'There is therefore an onus on professionals in all agencies to recognise and eradicate any underlying sexist stereotyping in the allocation of scarce resources' (BASW 1982:27.6, 61).

Where there is room for manoeuvre, social workers do have the opportunity to counteract sexist assumptions underlying the provision of community care. Social work practice from which gender-blindness has been erased ought to be engaging with issues about how that could be achieved.

'Growing older': images of the elderly in social work literature

Although the links between social work literature and social work practice may be tenuous at times, writing about social work at least gives some indication of the degree of sensitivity about gender issues that currently prevails. So how far is literature on social work practice with the elderly aware of gender divisions. Or does it reflect, and thus probably reinforce, gender-blindness?

In fact, the elderly as a topic hardly appears at all in social work literature, except in texts and articles that deal specifically with their needs (Rowlings 1981:131). Nor do the elderly feature in a recent text on 'radical' social work, that actually contains only one indexed reference to 'the elderly'. This concerns a half-page discussion about a social worker's attempt to obtain a telephone for an elderly woman (Bailey and Brake 1980:224–25). It seems that even those radical social workers who seek to challenge the terms in which social work is conventionally formulated have not yet found a place for work with the elderly in their radical alternatives.

Where the elderly do make an appearance, both ageist and sexist assumptions are to be found, singly and in combination. Rarely is account taken of the fact that the majority of the elderly are female, and that the sex imbalance is even more marked in the 'very old' population. A common and unisex image of the elderly is presented in terms of their 'infantile' qualities. Brearley, for instance, explicitly uses a model of childhood and an analogy of maternal deprivation to explain the response of some elderly people to admission to residential care (Brearley 1977:51–4) and elsewhere he argues that, 'If the baby can be the most powerful person in the household then so too can the frail elderly parent who may act out his [sic] infantile needs that have been under control for most of his life' (Brearley 1975:45).

This analogy with childhood serves to reinforce the notion that a client's age is, *per se*, his or her most significant identifying feature. This equation of the elderly with the young is widely used in social interaction and in language, and perhaps is best encapsulated in the commonly used phrase 'old boy' or 'old girl' to refer to an elderly person. In so far as social workers draw upon this kind of imagery when they deal with old people, they are in danger of perpetuating an uncritical and objectionable form of ageism in their contacts with elderly clients. Such ageism further disadvantages single women, for whom convention dictates a juvenile mode of address right on into extreme old age.

Social work texts abound with examples of sexism in the use of language about the elderly, including the BASW guidelines that follow what appears to be standard procedure in discussion of social work with the elderly, by referring to elderly users of social work services solely by the male gender, despite the reality that most are women (BASW 1977). Social workers, however, are usually assumed to be female. Perhaps the most blatant example is the title of Goldberg's discussion which, although centrally concerned with the elderly, could still be called 'Social Work Since Seebohm: All Things To All Men' (Goldberg 1979).

Discussions of the life situations of elderly clients *as women* are virtually absent from the literature of social work, while conventional gender assumptions are faithfully reflected, not challenged. An example of good social work practice with an elderly female client is given.

'Recognising that an old lady was totally discouraged, feeling useless with no contribution to make, the social worker would find small ways of helping her to regain some sense of worth and use, if only learning again how to do some simple knitting.'
(Goldberg *et al.* 1970:110–11)

Social workers as well as clients are subject to stereotyped gender assumptions,

'It is possible that very elderly women [clients] when faced with a modern young man were more difficult and hostile in their attitudes and generally less responsive than to a maternal-looking, middle aged woman social worker who could enter more naturally into their feminine pre-occupations.'   (Goldberg *et al.* 1970:102)

While it may be unfair to quote examples from a study that is more than a decade old, there appears to be no evidence in more recent social work literature of specific attempts to counteract and overcome sexist and ageist assumptions. If individual social workers are in fact attempting to do this in their own practice, it would seem that they receive little help from those who write about social work.

Another feature of the literature on social work with the elderly is its unquestioned assumptions about family status. Despite evidence to the contrary, the practical and moral superiority of living arrangements based on the nuclear family are upheld (Hugman 1981). The single (never-married) elderly, when they appear, are portrayed as lonely, isolated and above all, *deprived*: 'Those who have not been married are normally deprived of the support of children' (Brearley 1975:46). Brearley sees this presumed deprivation as, 'perhaps more significant for women than for men': as indeed it is, in terms of the practical consequences of lack of services that children might provide. The situation is presumably compounded for elderly childless women by their demonstrable failure to fulfil the central-life rationale that our culture accords women – the production of children. The consequences of this can be experienced as very real.

An Age Concern survey found that although elderly women living alone had as many friends as those who lived with other people, 'the advantage of having "all the good friends anyone could wish for" failed to match the advantages that come from living with a spouse, offspring or siblings' (Abrams 1980:59). Some of these elderly women may well have been dwelling on the prospect of an idealized family life, far removed from the reality experienced in households that incorporate family members. By contrast, a group of elderly women in hospital (most of whom lived alone) were vociferous in their wish for 'self-sufficiency' of a type that gives a degree of independence and autonomy (Cooper 1980:22) and showed disapproval of living with married children because 'women now worked very hard outside the home as well as inside it and had very little time'. Separate but near accommodation was the preferred choice in housing (Cooper 1980:68).

Widows appear in social work literature as lonely persons – a reality, no doubt, for those women who hitherto have defined themselves, and have had their married lifestyle defined for them, according to conventional criteria. Brearley portrays widows as tending,

> 'not to fit in with the married couples who had been friends. Unless the widowed person can find an acceptable partner, social inter-action outside the family becomes difficult because the number of social activities for single people is limited.'   (Brearley 1975:46)

Brearley's observation is correct, but his implied solution – remar-riage, is highly questionable, not least because with advancing old age there are far fewer men than women in the population and, in addition, the 'ideal' female marriage partner in our culture is younger than her husband.

It does seem that the cultural definition of women as having meaningful lives only through a domestic setting in which they service others does have the effect in old age of removing from frail elderly women who live alone the possibilities of investing life with real meaning. Nonetheless, the equation of living alone with a state of loneliness is challenged in the literature, for instance by Goldberg's findings that, 'living alone did not constitute quite such a hazard or source of unhappiness as is sometimes suggested' (Goldberg *et al.* 1970:57). Barker, in a sensitive article, emphasizes the importance of the satisfaction to be gained in old age from the friendship of those of a similar age who have shared similar life experiences. He argues that social work with the elderly should aim to ensure that elderly clients get into settings where such relationships can be formed and fostered (Barker 1980).

Thus, images of the elderly can be found in social work literature that: rarely take account of the fact that the majority of the very elderly are female, 'infantilize' elderly people, show examples of traditional gender behaviour as fostered by social workers, uphold living arrangements based on traditional family forms, and portray the stereotyped 'lonely widow'. In this, social work literature reflects much cultural imagery about elderly women, although occasional, more positive antidotes are to be found. Stearns reported that women were more adaptable than men to the state of being elderly, a state for which they 'seem to anticipate and plan' and 'to maintain a diversity of interest and pastimes, including varying degrees of domestic management' and to a lifestyle which, even if restricted in environ-ment and mobility, retained elements of choice and decision making.

While Stearns may appear to indicate that such elderly women are still stuck in the kitchen, he argues that 'they view their status and interests as more important than fulfilling a familial role' (Stearns 1977). Cooper agreed with this image of elderly women on the basis of her group work with elderly hospital patients (Cooper 1980).

By and large, however, women are excluded from social work literature; and where they become visible, they are discussed in ways that present no challenge at all to social work practices based on very conventional gender stereotypes.

Concluding remarks

What are the consequences for social work practice of the kinds of analysis that we have presented? First, it implies the need to question, and to move away from, thinking about work with the elderly that either treats elderly people as if they were all the same, ignoring significant differences between them, especially between men and women, or that operates on the basis of conventional stereotyped assumptions about gender differences. The implications extend not only to elderly clients, but also to those who care for many of them.

Second, breaking down those ways of thinking and working also involves breaking out of the limitations within which social work with the elderly is currently cast. If the elderly are seen as having more differentiated needs, then it follows that there must be a greater variety of ways to meet them. In particular, the profoundly ageist assumption that elderly clients are not suitable for receipt of the more complex and high-status skills that social workers have to offer, needs to be challenged. Many elderly people have to face life changes in old age that are more dramatic and far-reaching than any they have experienced before; there seems to be no case, therefore, for denying them the kind of assistance that might enable them not simply to accept changed circumstances, but to use them as positive opportunities for changes in their own lifestyle. As Brearley argues, 'Older people have a need for and a right to a choice of alternative lifestyles: they should be able to choose the kind of people they wish to be' (Brearley 1978:193). To deny them the kind of support that might facilitate such choices means that social workers are colluding with the social processes that effectively consign the elderly, most of whom it must be said again are women, to a kind of half life.

PART III ───────────

Towards feminist practice

6

Women and social work in Birmingham

THE BIRMINGHAM WOMEN AND SOCIAL WORK GROUP (81)

The Birmingham Women and Social Work Group started in May 1978. Most of us at that stage were students on a professional training course (CQSW) and were having difficulty reconciling what we were being taught with our experiences of social work agencies, and our politics. From its start our group has been based on our need as feminists to share our experiences, particularly those at the workplace. As the group has developed it has taken on other meanings and directions for us all, both collectively and individually. However, the most important change has been that each of us has experienced a deepened commitment to feminism. Consequently, we all know that an emerging feminist perspective in social work is crucial for the future of social work services that affect the lives of women.

Writing this chapter has posed many challenges to the group, but has proved useful in helping us define and describe both the theory and the practice of our politics. We have attempted first to locate our ideas of what a feminist social work practice should be in the economic climate of the 1980s – a climate of public-expenditure cuts and a grudging if not overtly antagonistic and censuring Welfare State. We go on to look at the elements of a feminist social work practice, how we relate to women clients, how we can use the Women's Movement as a resource – both for inspiration and practical help – and how we must take issue with some forms of radical social work in order to bring women's interests to the fore.

As 'the family', real or illusory, is still the major focus of social work intervention, we felt it necessary to comment on the type of repressive work with women who have family responsibilities that is currently engaged in by local authority social workers and probation officers. We attempt to pose some alternatives, particularly in child care and work with adolescent girls. Finally we discuss the perennial problem of how we work with men – clients, colleagues, managers, and trade unionists.

Developing theory

No one can be in any doubt that the last few years have seen a development of a feminist perspective of social work, beginning with the writings and conference workshops of Elizabeth Wilson in the early 1970s and the Feminism and Social Work Practice Conference at Warwick in 1979. Both played their part in bringing about further national conferences (Birmingham 1980; Bradford 1981; London 1982) where the development of a feminist perspective was placed firmly within the politics of the Women's Movement. The commitment shown at these conferences emphasized the importance and momentum of a feminist analysis.

Our commitment as a group is to share our experiences and to develop our ideas collectively, and is rooted in feminist politics as they have developed in recent years. Feminism has not simply concerned itself with objectively describing women's condition as an oppressed group, but with women's subjective experience of their subordination and oppression. It involves a recognition of the personal as political and stresses the importance of each woman's experience of oppression in developing ways of challenging that subordination.

This inclusion of the personal as a crucial part of feminist analysis means that the Women's Movement has had to seek new forms of political organization, a different idea of how theories should be developed and how we relate to theory. On the other hand, if we do not take into account the specific experiences of women, we may create a kind of feminist stereotype that does not relate to women's lives and which fails to reflect the ways in which oppression is internalized by the individual. We therefore have to develop new ways of conceptualizing our experiences and generalizing from them, so that our ideas can be shared with others and extended. For this to happen we have created a form of organizing as feminists, that is non-hierarchical and that allows us, as individuals, to contribute our experiences to the development of theory.

Although the starting point is always the same – a commitment to feminism – our developing theory is a dynamic process. All of our experiences are of crucial importance in producing and strengthening feminist theories that provide the support and opportunities we need to change ourselves. This method of developing theories challenges traditional ideas that theory is somehow handed down from above, such ideas are prevalent in many political groups and in the attitudes of many academics.

Having gone so far down this road of developing an analysis in the context of our politics, we now feel that it is important to define and describe our position, particularly as a result of the growing number of attempts to link feminism and social work. We challenge the notion that feminist theory can be synthesized and applied. It is clear that it is only as feminist workers that we can analyse, share, and set down our experiences as the beginnings of a feminist perspective. The commitment shown at the national conferences demonstrates that feminist workers can use their experiences to build a political analysis. Clearly though, feminist workers need researchers and academics, for they have the information skills and access to resources that are important. Feminists in whatever sphere have contributions to make. But we are among a number of women who feel that the relationship between academics and a feminist perspective of social work must be viewed with care. We are concerned that feminism will become the next social work bandwagon. Should this happen, a new social work theory (a library shelf labelled Feminism, cosily sandwiched between Family Therapy and Freud?) will be the final outcome, rather than a political analysis of women's experiences. It would then be a short step to the institutionalization of feminism. If social workers and social work training courses are to take seriously the contribution of feminism to their practice, they must do so in ways that do not ignore its dynamism and creativity, its crucially challenging and questioning nature, and how feminism is lived by women and how it affects our lives.

While the pressures on us as a group to be active are enormous, we have found that it has become important to create opportunities for making a written contribution to the developing feminist perspective on social work. We believe that such a perspective must include our personal experiences of work, and that unless feminist social workers take on the task of recording their experiences the content and direction of the feminist perspective will not reflect our concerns. If this proves to be the case the power and potential impact of our political analysis and practice will be lost.

Working within the state

Our feminism affects our attitudes towards working within the state. We believe that in the past socialists have tended to make a simplistic analysis of the state's involvement in our lives, seeing it both as a neutral force on which we can make demands, *and* (as with radical social work) as a directly coercive force. The Women's Movement and the understanding generated by our fight against public expenditure cuts have challenged these perspectives.

Our interaction with the state is contradictory. On the one hand we need many of the benefits the state provides (for example, social security payments, health care) but on the other hand people, and particularly women seeking welfare services, are often involved in oppressive relationships that define them as 'inadequate', or 'scroungers'. In fighting the cuts our understanding of the contradictions have increased, and all too often we have found ourselves defending services that we know to be oppressive and inadequate. We have had difficulty in developing a strategy that allows us to defend existing services, while fighting for the kinds of provision needed. But it is clearly important not just to consider what the state does, but also how it relates to people and the nature of social relationships it produces. A patriarchal society is one founded on male dominance and it attributes a fixed set of characteristics to people on the basis of their sex. Therefore, the Welfare State cannot be neutral because it has been constructed to reflect patriarchal social relationships. As Wilson has put it: 'One way of looking at social policy would be to describe it as a set of structures created by men to shape the lives of women' (Wilson 1983b:33).

This view of the state has particular implications for us as feminist social workers. Social work is often the place where the state meets the individual and defines her needs and problems. We want to see ourselves as social workers who are trying to help people, but all too often we find ourselves exercising an oppressive control over individuals' lives. All social work takes place on the basis of underlying values, which, all too often, are not recognized. As feminists we try to state our values and use them in our work.

The values and ideas that come from our feminism also suggest ways in which we can work from within existing state institutions, for different forms of social relationships in order to provide a basis for new kinds of relationships with the recipients of our services. The attempt to develop sharing and less oppressive relationships with our clients has been one of the aims of our group.

So what are the principles of feminist social work? We must acknowledge first of all that we live in a patriarchal society. The struggles against oppression based on race and class are crucial, but in different ways. Women's opposition to patriarchy has neither an immediate parallel in the fight for socialism, nor reliable allies in male socialists, black or white.

As social workers we work predominantly with women. Many of the problems that bring them to us are inextricably bound up with the roles assigned to women in our society and the impossible strains, both physical and emotional, that are their life experiences. As women we have experiences in common that we can share and explore with our women clients. A fundamental principle of the Women's Liberation Movement is that the personal is the political. When we confront our clients with the detail of their daily lives, we are handling potential dynamite.

The textbook social worker – who empathizes with clients but does not get 'involved', who 'facilitates' them in the direction of change, but does not search in her own experience to see how painful and frightening change can be, and who never raises politics for fear of management retribution, is not helping her women clients to understand and transform their lives. Feminism is both a personal and political commitment. As such it cannot be alternatively utilized or discarded on a whim – we have to live it.

Discussing political questions with our clients comes easily, they inevitably arise in the course of reflection about relationships and activities that are proving difficult. In our experience there are few women who are unwilling to talk about and, indeed, query their natural role as caretakers of children, the sick, their menfolk, the elderly. And there are few elderly women who are not aware that society loses interest in them once their 'servicing' days are over.

While we can use our feminism as a direct approach to women, it would clearly be naïve to claim immediate and unconditional rapport with all women on the basis of our common experience of living in a male-dominated world. We acknowledge that as mainly white, middle-class, salaried women we are distanced from many of our clients. The power vested in us to make decisions about other people's lives also sets us apart. We can only hope that our feminist principles give us extra sensitivity and prevent us from being dishonest about our power, or using it as a basis for patronizing other women (the male language does seem particularly appropriate here).

Consciousness raising has always been and will continue to be a crucial activity within the Women's Movement. We would regard much of our work with women as being consciousness raising, not so much in the sense of setting up groups specifically for this purpose but as a description of the type of dialogue we enter into with women, both on a one-to-one basis and in various types of activity group (for example, Intermediate Treatment groups). Most women *are* aware of their oppression, but many do not feel able to fight it. The purpose of consciousness raising is to explore our experience of being women and most importantly to validate it to ourselves and formulate the possibilities of change. This is a dynamic process that does not end. We do not develop to a 'correct' level of feminist consciousness, nor is one woman's experience more valid than another's. The rooting out of the patriarchal ideology that serves as a viciously distorting filter to our self-image and understanding of life in general, is not something we can do to or for other women without being involved ourselves and exploring our own vulnerability.

The casework relationship has been much derided by radical social workers as oppressive, pseudo-psychoanalytic, leading to the locating of problems within individuals, rather than in social structures. One-to-one work can be all these things but need not be. Sexism is a social structure and has to be opposed by a variety of political strategies and tactics, including the tackling of feelings about ourselves. These are often personal and very painful, but nonetheless crippling for us, unless we learn to share them. We would aim, where possible, to involve women in groups where they could offer one another support and affection. However, while groups engage some women, they equally silence and intimidate others. The value and necessity of working individually with certain women should not be underestimated. An essential principle of feminist social work should be that we do not ask more of other women than we ask of ourselves, whether it be joining groups to share experiences or making practical changes in lifestyles. Social workers are notoriously good at thinking they know what is best for other people. Self-scrutiny could prevent us recommending changes to women that we know we could not handle without the back-up of our sisters in the Women's Movement. For example, all too often we hear social workers recommending glibly to battered women that they forsake their partner of twenty years, seek injunctions, set up on their own, find themselves a social life and a job – as if it were just a simple remedy to a straightforward problem!

One of the most important things we can offer women is support. In terms of consciousness raising, much of our most effective and positive work has been our involvement in the routine, bread-and-butter work of our departments – supporting a woman whose supplementary benefit was withdrawn on grounds of alleged cohabitation, through humiliating interrogations by DHSS officers and a hopeless appeal to a Tribunal; working with depressed and isolated lone mothers; talking to adolescent girls whose behaviour classes them as 'beyond control'. These are overtly political problems and should be addressed as such. Working with women towards a greater understanding of the forces in our society that operate against our common interests is a political activity (Jordan and Parton 1983).

The ideas, support, and resources of the wider Women's Movement are essential to the development of feminist social work. The value of what the state provides for women needs to be questioned. Health and child care facilities, for example, are often inadequate, alienating, and offered grudgingly. Calls for women's control over the services supposedly provided *for* them by the state have fallen on stony ground and women have learnt from bitter experience that the state cannot be relied upon to provide a facility that does not have a sting in its tail. Yes, local authorities have day nurseries, but so few that the only way to guarantee a place is to threaten to batter the child. Thus the mother, and not the lack of services, becomes the problem!

Alternative resources set up by women and for women are invaluable, not only because we can refer our clients to them for specific types of help and support, but also because they serve as models for the future development of state services. These resources provide an example of the type of services we would want in terms of both focus and organization, being collectively run and non-repressive in approach. As social workers many of us have chosen to work within the state, but as feminists we inevitably work critically and seek to change the many oppressive ways in which the state operates, particularly towards girls and women. Women's Aid and the Rape Crisis Centres stand out as self-help groups that have forced general recognition of a universal problem – male violence to women – and have had some impact on policy, for example: local authority housing provision for battered women. Women's Centres, Pregnancy Testing Services, pregnancy advisory agencies, women and health groups, Women's Therapy Centres, and many others, similarly present a challenge to the state's definitions and priorities, and explicitly reject the controlling male hand in their activities. The Welfare State is of crucial concern to feminists. Constant dialogue with our sisters in the wider Women's Movement should help to ensure that the issues around welfare provision taken up by Women's Liberation correspond to the needs of our women clients and engage them as much as possible. The campaign and debates of the Women's Movement also fuel the struggles we, as state employees, wage from within.

Our approach to Politics (capital 'P', rather than the politics of personal life) has developed out of the recognition that women's oppression arises from a structural inequality in society, which is not necessarily combated by adopting the theories and tactics of the left. Our wish not to be too closely linked with radical social work stems from this. Our roots are securely anchored in the Women's Movement, though this obviously does not preclude many of us from regarding ourselves as socialists also.

The early radical social workers aligned themselves in unequivocal opposition to the monolithic state (Corrigan and Leonard 1978). They worked from 'outposts', such as advice and community centres, and only reluctantly admitted by whom they were paid. They talked of the interests of the working class, the Revolution, the Workers' State, and either failed to see or chose to ignore the fact that male revolutionary heroes in the privacy of their homes sometimes beat up their wives. Women simply cannot afford to hang on in the hope that 'the Revolution' will liberate them, along with the working class. We have our own war to fight and it starts long before we get to the trade union meeting or housing action group.

More recent attempts to re-appraise radical social work see contra-dictions in the state and are ready to accept that we can work both 'in and against' it (Glasgow Weekend Group 1980). The particular oppression of women is now acknowledged but, disappointingly, the remedy remains much the same – organize within your union, join a political party, bring your politics into the male-dominated structures of the Left, and 'We'll see you right sister!' Of course we must use all available channels to raise women's questions and make demands of our potential political allies, but *how* we raise these questions and *how* we choose to fight will inevitably influence the type and quality of any change we bring about. The strategies that we have chosen to adopt are discussed later in this chapter.

For feminists the scope of political inquiry is infinitely wide and by necessity creative. Not only do we have to push out the frontiers, we also have to delve into the past and decide what is useful to us. As feminist social workers an important task is to plough through both the established and the fringe theories and practices to see what can be reworked to the advantage of women. Community work is an interesting example. Radical social workers have been ambivalent towards it. When they were 'outposted' the community was of obvious significance as the site for developing an oppositional power base. Later the whole concept of the community was called into question as social scientists, among others, pointed out how many aspects of so-called community life were controlled from elsewhere and were therefore difficult to influence: for example, the Community Development Projects. We would argue that for women the commu-nity can be central, mainly because of their caretaking role. Women with children spend a lot of time going to and fro in their locality, from school to home, to the shops, to the doctor's, to the playgroup. If they work it is likely to be in the vicinity so that they can mini-mize travelling time and be at home early to prepare for their returning families. In this context, organizing a children's play scheme can be a highly charged political activity, as it directly challenges women's role as the primary caretakers of children (Mayo 1977).

We must constantly ask ourselves in whose interests we are acting, and we must check with each other, our clients, and our sisters elsewhere that we are not backsliding into the view that women's battles can be fought for them, rather than by them.

Working with the family

It is widely assumed by welfare agencies and governments that the stereotypical nuclear family (breadwinner father, dependent mother and 2.4 children) is the commonest and most effective institution for the care and upbringing of children. This assumption is inaccurate (Statham 1978; Rimmer 1981; Rapaport and Fogarty 1982). Social workers find themselves working with single parents, children in residential homes, young people on their own, the elderly, women alone supporting sick and dependent adults, and the homeless. This fact requires a more realistic recognition of the varied nature of domestic life and methods of working that reflect this. What is more, we would reject the related assumption that the nuclear family is ideal and naturally healthy. Our politics provides the basis for analysing those destructive pressures that lead to the public symptoms of distress and conflict that we are required to deal with. Those symptoms are found in middle-class nuclear households and are not unique to so-called 'broken homes'. Raising children in the family is extremely difficult both practically and emotionally. What must be argued for is a much more flexible, resourceful, and responsive range of child care provision, with a strong commitment to public expenditure.

Nevertheless, we are ultimately faced with the fact that the concept of the family is central to social work theory and practice, as well as having a key position in the thinking and policy making of successive governments. In the post-war years the majority of social policy has been concerned with maintaining the stability of the family as an institution, with very little attention being paid to the quality of family life. All governments have been nervous about what they see as the possible disintegration of the family. This anxiety is manifested in, for example, the interest paid to increasing divorce rates and the incidence of single parenthood, and in calls to create a Minister for the Family. The fact that the nuclear family is so often seen as the only viable and acceptable way of life means that social work and welfare policies only aim to maintain this system or cope with its failures. By using the notion of the nuclear family as the starting point for analysis, policies are designed according to an inaccurate view of the way people live, and services are set up that are inappropriate to its needs (Segal 1983).

For example, the DHSS's cohabitation laws and the forgoing of the right of a woman to claim supplementary benefit if her boyfriend or husband is working or claiming or seen to be part of the family unit, presuppose that the male automatically takes on the role of bread-winner and head of the family. Our view is that we should be making allegiances with other agencies, both statutory and voluntary, to try to change both this policy and its supporting ideology. At the same time, a priority must be to work with women who suffer as a result of such policies. Supporting a woman who is making an appeal at a DHSS tribunal is as crucial as fighting the inequities on a broader political front.

Scares about 'latch-key' children, 'hooliganism', increasing num-bers of adolescents coming before the courts, and general concern for law and order, combined with massive cuts in public expenditure, have meant that the family, and more specifically women, are being called on to fill the gaps. The emphasis of current mainstream social work practice is about keeping families together, without recognizing how oppressive this can be for the woman. In practice it is the woman, in her role as unpaid worker, who is being asked to be geriatric nurse, nursery teacher, social worker, and health visitor. Many social workers support a view of the family as an important and vital unit for people's well-being, without looking at who bears the cost of this 'security' and 'stability' – women.

When the family is unable to carry out the tasks without assistance, the state has to step in. As social workers it is crucial that we should realize the role the state creates for us in upholding the family. Indeed, this is one area when our work within the state shows the contradic-tions and tensions we face. As feminists we are aware of the subordi-nate position of women in this analysis of welfare, and the direct role played by the state in women's oppression. State benefits, such as family income supplement, are aimed at bolstering the family house-hold system and women are seen as servicers of wage-earning men (Land 1978). Of relevance for us is that when the state steps in to carry out service tasks – from home-help to residential care for children – it does so in such a way that it is seen as taking over functions properly belonging to the family, or substituting for work that 'should' be done by housewives (Davis 1981).

Very little is said on most social work courses about how notions of the family and the role of women within it are moulded by the patriarchal nature of contemporary society. Indeed, there is very little material that deals specifically with the relationship between women and welfare, and this in itself reflects the limits of social work focus and its dependence on patriarchy. Social work ideology is patriarchal ideology and patriarchy is not something 'out there'. Most social work courses continue to transmit the ideology of the family as basically good and necessary, and sidestep the issues that we are attempting to raise. The potential contribution of feminism towards a critical analysis of social work theory in this area is very great.

In addition to the tensions and contradictions in our work within the state, we also face our own personal dilemmas in our thinking about the family. Some of us are married or living with men, some of us have children. The family is complex and ambiguous. It can be both good and bad – a place where we experience caring, loving relationships, but also a destructive, oppressive force in our lives. This is as true for us as it is for our clients. To mask from our clients our own experiences would be dishonest. We should not expect our clients to bare their deepest thoughts and frustrations while we sympathize from within a sterile bubble. We clearly cannot resolve all these dilemmas, but as feminists we need at least to challenge existing social work thinking and teaching on the family, straitjacketed as it is. It can be difficult to do this if you are isolated or low down the rung in the office power structure, but even a brief look at some of the bread and butter of our work shows areas we are concerned about.

Family therapy, emergency crisis work to prevent families breaking up, and payments to families (from section 1 of the Children and Young Persons Act 1963) are only some examples of the ways in which social workers seek to help families stay together. There is an enormous amount of pressure for parents to perform. An example of this is rehabilitating a child from care. Social services departments require the parents' agreement for a child to go 'home on trial'. By this means the parents are prepared to accept the disciplinary and nurturing role. Agencies other than our employer's make demands on us and our clients to conform, for example: Family Service Units, Intermediate Treatment centres, Child Guidance clinics and hospitals. They will often refuse to work with children as individuals without involving the family actively and making judgements about parents not supporting or controlling children appropriately. While we want to work with families as well as children on their own, we would want to see such work in terms of a more critical approach to the value of the family unit, and a recognition that in some instances the family is beyond repair, and that this breakdown is not necessarily due to failure on the parents' part.

In spite of efforts to keep families together, we have to make quick, difficult decisions. Removing children from their families is contradictory work. When it comes to the crunch we find it as difficult as any other social worker and we are conscious of the ambivalence in ourselves. Therefore, we have to begin with ourselves and analyse our position. We must acknowledge the fact that the family can be a nasty and violent place to be, and we do not want to see women and children badly treated, but we must work towards family members relating in a different way. In Birmingham, to receive a child into care is no longer simply the social worker's decision. Bureaucratic procedures seem to dominate. Cuts have meant closure of children's homes in order to reduce the number of children coming into care, and foster parents have been recruited to ensure the child has an alternative family to go to.

We would like to see a more flexible approach to family difficulties and breakdown. Women should be able to choose what hours they need for the care of children, so that they do not feel inadequate by being told that social workers can do better. It is not easy to argue for this flexibility but an example of an achievement here was that we persuaded a residential nursery to sleep a baby and to allow the mother to care for the child during the day. Community-based short-term residential care, week or day care for children that does not 'institutionalize' them, must be seen as innovative. It is possible, and currently practised in a Birmingham home, to share the care of difficult adolescents with their parents, as opposed to substituting their care entirely. For instance, a child may spend all week at a children's home, while another is admitted to care at weekends. The arrangement made is dependent on the family situation and in this way caring is shared with parents on an agreed basis.

When cases are allocated to social workers we often hear 'he needs a father figure' or 'this child needs a woman social worker who can be a mother to him or her'. Women's groups are often run, not to raise consciousness but to encourage women to be 'better mothers; to learn to play with their children', thus ensuring that the position of the woman in the family is maintained, and that she will continue to provide all those services that are required of her. The father is rarely included in 'better parenting'. While it is assumed that 'poor mother-ing' is a failure of the woman and is a risk to her children, no such heavy burdens are placed on the father, whose role is usually seen as an economic one. Women who need a way out of an oppressive or destructive family face both heavy judgements and practical barriers. The struggles battered women have in being treated seriously when they ask for alternative housing and benefit in their own right is just one example. Our connection with the wider Women's Movement gives us access to resources that are provided for women by women and are more sensitive to women's needs. For instance Women's Aid's hostels offer more support, less humiliation, and no offensive ques-tioning, compared with the punitive nature of Housing Department hostels.

Probation officers, working with 'prisoners' wives and families', are in an ambivalent position. On the one hand the women are single, while on the other hand they are without any of the freedoms or status that implies. Probation officers have a primary responsibility to the prisoner. Therefore, work with the woman will tend to be in her role as wife and mother. It is difficult for probation officers to be honest in this situation as the concern is to 'keep the home together' for the prisoner's eventual release. Other problems are encountered when working with adult women who offend. They are usually also wives or girlfriends and often mothers. Because of their role within the family they tend to be seen in this context, rather than as individuals. This contrasts with work with male offenders where far more emphasis is placed on them as individuals and on structural factors, such as employment. Writing Social Enquiry Reports can draw us into pushing stereotyped images of women in order to get the 'best deal' for a particular offender. There is a tendency to emphasize aspects of her domestic situation, like her ability to provide for her children, and this may often be used to explain her appearance in court as unusual (Worrall 1981). The family is a crucial influence on our clients, and we must acknowledge this without retreating into 'old fashioned' notions of casework.

Working with individual women we hope we empathize with their experiences as women, whether or not they have children. We try not to criticize them as mothers or carers, but we must acknowledge the fact that we do have power – to supervise children on care orders, and if necessary remove them from the home, or arrange alternative care for adult relatives. We want to share our experience as feminists, and be honest with the women we work with. Women's groups we are involved with do not concentrate on women being better mothers, but challenge the oppression that many women experience in the family. We provide access to advice and information, have discussions, encourage mutual support. We try to increase women's awareness of their position in society, and give them confidence to fight their oppression.

In our work with adolescent girls, the dilemma of the feminist social worker is seen quite clearly, both in social work theory and practice. Few researchers of juvenile delinquency examine the subject of girls. When they are dealt with it is usually superficially or in relation to boys. There is an overt acceptance that boys will be boys but girls will be disturbed. Girls have been written out of delinquency theory because they are often considered mad not bad. In much of the better known work, delinquent behaviour in boys is seen as an extension of their exuberant, boisterous predispositions. It is interpreted as their striving towards self-assertion or as an attempt to conform to peer group pressures. Most theory emphasizes the transitory nature of such behaviour, for instance: most boys 'grow out' of their criminal tendencies in their early twenties. There is no attempt to define masculine behaviour as a problem in itself. By contrast, female juvenile delinquency is often thought to be linked with poor parenting. As such, it is feared that its effects will be felt for longer and will be 'transmitted' to successive generations when the girls become mothers. The cycle of deprivation model tends to play a much larger part in this explanation. It could be argued that there is some advantage to the fact that girls have been ignored by delinquency theories. However, it must be remembered that this does not mean that girls are excluded from the juvenile-court system. Indeed, girls are frequently referred to the courts as being 'beyond control' or in 'moral danger'. Such labels are infinitely more stigmatizing and far-reaching than the criminal offences for which boys are brought to the juvenile courts. Additionally, these labels are often attached to girls even when their appearance in court is due directly to a criminal offence. Very little research has been conducted specifically about female crime and what little there has been has concentrated on the personal pathology model. Feminist researchers such as Carol Smart (Smart 1978) are now beginning to touch on this important subject, using a different set of assumptions about the explanations of female crime.

Creating alternatives

Somehow the feminist social worker must attempt to redress the balance caused by a powerful input from the family, other agencies, and the media that militate against helping adolescent girls to understand the way their role in society is being defined and maintained.

Women in our group have already established 'girls only' nights in youth clubs and now there is an increasing trend in Intermediate Treatment work to provide this facility. However, quite often the way girls choose to rebel takes the form of enlightened 'femaleness' and sexuality. In schools, girls replace the preferred image of neatness, passivity, and conscientiousness with a more sexual one – wearing make-up to school, 'flirting with boys' – in an attempt to challenge the authority of the school. Early marriage, fashion, and beauty all become part of the anti-school culture, but in adopting these lines of rebellion they are actually contributing to their own oppression.

Girls only groups are currently seen as an oddity, the results of which are not taken seriously by social work managers or colleagues, until they threaten the established norms of family casework. It is difficult to see how girls groups can get away from this experimental image. The groups often have to be forced into existence as a kind of positive discrimination. They are set up, at worst, usually with initial resistance, or at best, curiosity from the girls themselves. This may be due to historical factors, in that men, at the workplace and in social life, are encouraged to combine in groups, while the woman's place is traditionally in the home. This has left them more isolated and less able to form such groups. This situation is reinforced in the youth subculture. Boys combine in larger groups, for instance, to play organized games. Girls generally tend to combine in small groups of two or three. In the boyfriend/girlfriend arena, where girls wait passively, it is often thought easier for girls to 'get off' with boys in these smaller associations. Additionally, the hinterland in which adolescents operate is considerably smaller for girls. A pertinent example is the ways in which adolescents earn their pocket money. Boys tend to get Saturday jobs or paper rounds, which take them outside the immediate influence of the family, while girls tend to earn their money baby sitting or doing housework in the home. Their extra-curricular activities are more firmly based within the home. The best friend and confidante, therefore, affords more importance in their lives.

The avenues open to working-class girls to attain some measure of independence from family life are limited. Girls rarely leave the family home before marriage or cohabitation and the setting up of a family. The goal of many girls is marriage and a family – not to achieve this by their late twenties is construed as being 'left on the shelf'. Boys, on the other hand, learn that independence and freedom are essential before settling down. Their sexual, social, and economic freedom once gained, ensures that, to a great extent, men retain independence and power over women in marriage. This patriarchal status is not earned; men see it as their right.

As many of the workers who set up girls groups, we have had different life experiences from the girls. We have been encouraged to seek careers and attain financial independence, if only as an interim measure. The majority of us have at one time been to college, where 'settling down' is considered unwise, and where we have had the time and personal space to experiment and explore our independence in many ways. The difference in experience has been highlighted in many of the girls groups we have run. Some sessions included activities that were alien to most of the girls. For instance, with one group, a session was set aside to go for a hamburger in the city centre. Although the previous weeks had been marked by high attendance figures, nobody turned up at the meeting place for the meal. This type of experience was new to the girls, and few of them had the confidence to handle it. For the workers, however, this activity was not difficult or threatening. The lesson we learnt was that we must be constantly aware of such differences, and ensure that we start from the same position as the girls.

Perhaps a more important and difficult aspect to deal with is the differing attitudes and norms relating to pre-marital sex and contraception. For many of the girls we work with, 'pre-marital' sex is seen as just that: it must be seen in terms of true love and eventual marriage. To experience intercourse in any other context is frowned upon. Pre-marital sex must also be seen to be unprepared, an uncontrollable passion of the moment. Hence, the attitude towards effective contraception is ambivalent. For a girl to go out prepared for sex is interpreted as brazen. It puts her in the role of the hunter rather than the hunted – she is 'looking for it'.

Within the context of a girls group these attitudes can be explored and analysed by the girls themselves. This process begins with the setting up of the girls only group. The exclusion of boys in itself is instrumental in stimulating the group, and perceiving the difference it makes to the way the girls interact. They quickly overcome any misgivings or nervousness about being in an all female social situation and patently don't experience the indecisiveness and disinterestedness that is often attributed to them in mixed company. Varied programmes including discussion (on sex and relationships, school, employment prospects, motherhood) and physical activities (self-defence is ideal for raising issues as well as being of practical use) give them the chance to experiment with their bodies and their minds, and also develop a sense of identity of themselves as young women. A main aim of this type of work is to show girls that their futures are not pre-ordained – a job, if they can get one, need not just be a stopgap before the inevitable marriage.

Finally, the expectations of other referring agencies often cause tensions when setting up feminist groups. After all, girls groups are not intrinsically feminist. Colleagues often refer girls who, they say, need help with their 'personal appearance', are 'beyond control', in 'moral danger' and so on. They then wait to see if their clients emerge as feminine paragons of innocence who strive towards female compliance and acceptance of their lot in society. This brings into question the whole issue of how to measure the success of a group. As most girls who are referred to social work agency groups are seen to be deviant, they must be seen to be conformist when they emerge from the group. Setting up a girls group with strong feminist aims cannot fulfil this role. The aim should be: to help the girls to challenge critically society's view of themselves, to help them come to a better understanding of the forces operating around them, and to lift themselves out of the status quo of subordination and acceptance of their lot. Whether this goal can be achieved entirely within the context of girls groups is highly questionable, but no one can deny that it is at least a starting point.

As feminists we are working within state structures that aim to define, limit, and control women. We are striving to create new forms that will mean departing partially or totally from existing radical or traditional ways of working and organizing. It is important, therefore, to share our knowledge and experience in group or one-to-one work with women.

Working with men

It must be acknowledged that until we started organizing our thoughts to write this chapter we had not attempted to develop a substantial analysis of working with men, either as clients or as colleagues. Our concern is with women. But we cannot ignore the fact that we work alongside men in male-dominated organizations. The frustrations, anger, and difficulties we have all encountered have been discussed in the group, the focus being on personal experiences of facing suspicion, prejudice, hostility, and the various 'interpretations' of our behaviour that have been foisted on us. We face the same attitudes and prejudices as feminists in any job, when our politics are openly stated. However, we feel that we face particular problems because of the nature of our work. Suspicion and fear about the relationships we are attempting to establish with women clients do exist. Accusations are made that because we fight for women's rights we cannot make 'objective' assessments about women, particularly on how they fulfil their traditional role – child care and housekeeping. We face the accusations (couched in good social work terms) that we are rebelling against our sexuality, acting out our fantasies through women, and forcing women to conform to our beliefs and values. We do not deny that our politics and our jobs create tensions for us, but to be faced with attitudes that range from the patronizing to the hostile is a daily experience that we all find frustrating, and at times painful. The support we have gained from taking these experiences back to our group cannot be over emphasized.

However, we all feel that we must use our experience of working with male colleagues, and male clients, to build a wider analysis of our position as feminist workers. Our lives and our women clients' lives are affected and constrained by men, and in order to understand our experiences in social work agencies we need to understand the position of male workers, particularly from a historical perspective.

Social work has its roots in middle-class philanthropy and the workers (as opposed to the holders of resources) have traditionally been women – extending their caring roles from the home into the community. In the last decade the idea of social work as a profession has grown in importance. The increase in the number of male social workers has been a partial cause and result of this growth. The so-called 'rediscovery of poverty' in the early 1960s, coupled with the liberal attitudes prevalent at the time, attracted men (as well as women) to social work as a career. A career that involved helping the poor and dispossessed but did not mean direct involvement in the capitalist 'rat race'. A job that offered reasonable remuneration, security, and the possibility of advancement (however limited) is always an attractive proposition, yet basic-grade social work revolves around caring and supporting people, often women. Why do men become social workers? How do they see their role? Men are not of course innately incapable of taking on a caring role but they are rarely socialized into it. Conventions of male behaviour allow little space for intimate and emotional interactions with each other. Men are accustomed to the caring and supporting in a family being undertaken by women. There must be contradictions and tensions in male workers when they pass judgements on women (their child care and housekeeping standards).

It is in residential work that the roles played in society are most clearly replicated. Children's homes are very often headed by men who can exert their physical power as a means of control. Children and staff alike are seen to be dependent on them for guidance and leadership. Few men choose to become domestic workers or care assistants in old people's homes or home-helps – directly caring and practical jobs. Such choice maintains the sexual hierarchy. We regret that we see little evidence that the majority of male workers acknowledge the contradictions inherent in their role. There is a small and increasing number of male workers who subscribe to the basic demands of the Women's Liberation Movement. While welcoming this trend we must retain a degree of scepticism. How great is their commitment to change in their own lives? Are they really offering to renounce their social, economic, political, and sexual power? What sort of work do they engage in with their women clients? We feel that the reasons that men are not experiencing the contradictions and tensions inherent in their role (or at least not acknowledging them) lie partly in the redefinitions of the social work task that have taken place over the last two decades. First, social work has been made into a more academically respectable subject, using 'scientific' jargon – a trend reflected in and confirmed by the expansion of social work training courses, many leading to the award of MA or MSc degrees. Second, the large welfare bureaucracies that mushroomed with the development of generic social services departments (Seebohm restructuring) have created an attractive career path for men in social work, away from caring and into the management of staff and the control of resources. In both social services and probation there are vastly disproportionate numbers of men in higher grades compared to the number in these services as a whole. There are a multitude of reasons for this, not least being active discrimination against women seeking promotion. Social expectations lead men to see social work as a career in which they expect to get on. And so it is likely that many feel more fulfilled in management roles than as grass roots workers.

Thus the policy and practice of our workplace is largely determined by men. As the present Government goes ahead with its steady dismantling of the Welfare State, local decisions on where the cuts will be made, which sections of the service can be sacrificed, are made by predominantly male management bodies. Their definition of priorities frequently shows a lack of understanding or regard for the dramatic repercussions on women's lives. Those of us who are probation officers are faced with the effects of the Government's Law and Order lobby. Priority is being given to more controlling sentences rather than preventive work. While we would support, in principle, alternatives to custodial sentences such as Community Service Orders, these are being developed at the expense of very necessary supportive work with families. For example, women struggling to manage while their partners are in prison are not being given priority in terms of our agency's workload. In social services departments there is a drive back to 'community care' – for example, fostering not just of children but of the mentally handicapped and elderly. In practice this means additional burdens for women, whose caring role is usually undervalued and inadequately financed (EOC 1981; Finch and Groves 1983). The reality is that caring still falls upon women, and the effect of these changes is to increase the oppression of women.

Because local decisions like these, taken by our male-dominated managements, have crucial implications for us and the lives of women clients, we need to work to influence them. Our group made representations to the Birmingham Child Care Review Group. This all male committee, apparently unaware of the absence of a female member until we pointed it out to them, were looking at all child care services in the city of Birmingham with a view to making radical and sweeping changes. We took the opportunity to attempt to influence its decisions because we were not convinced that submissions by local union branches would address themselves to the issues satisfactorily.

As we find ourselves with an increasing amount of basic-grade social work experience, we are faced with the age-old dilemma of whether we should be seeking promotion. Can we influence at the grass roots level? And if not, do we have to emulate men in order to attain positions of power? We know that as men reach positions of power, the skills needed to attain these positions are redefined. The effect of this is to close the door even more firmly in the face of those people who wish to attain those positions, and bring about change in the organization, but who see the social work task in a different way. If we decide to opt for promotion as a means of bringing about changes (that is if we have not entirely disqualified ourselves by being known to hold 'radical' views) what then? The newly promoted social worker will find herself isolated in a male-dominated management team where her ability to manage is judged by men. She will probably face great suspicion from her male colleagues as a woman in an incongruous position. The only way to survive may be to be 'one of the lads'. Unfortunately, the success of one woman in management does not necessarily pave the way for others (Popplestone 1980).

Attitudes are such that a successful woman is seen as atypical. Additionally, a successful career may be gained at considerable personal loss. Women are often faced with the choice of career or family, whereas men are automatically assumed to have the right to move up the ladder and have families, while being nurtured by women. Our agencies do make the necessary statutory provision, for example, maternity leave. However, we should be demanding that further provision is made, to support the large number of women social workers with dependents. Such provisions are unlikely to be offered to us; we must force the decision and shape the kind of provisions developed according to our needs.

One way in which we can exert influence in our agencies is through unions. However, the unions too are male dominated, and female power and influence is less than their proportionate membership should suggest. Union organization and language are often alien to women. Debating is an activity more familiar to men and strange to women who are used to talking informally on the basis of personal experience.

It is vitally important that women do exert influence on their unions and make them work for themselves and their sisters. We have found that to discuss issues in the group until we are strong and confident to speak on them at union meetings has been of great value. Some unions have women's caucases where members can gain support to exert influence on the wider membership. This is important if we are to face and tackle the sexist attitudes of our colleagues and force recognition of the personal and the political issues (for example, sexual harassment at work, crèche facilities).

Our participation in political debates and campaigns on housing, unemployment, poverty, and the cuts is crucially informed by the particular needs of women. The cry from the unions for more houses, jobs, and money is insufficient for us. We must argue for qualitative as well as quantitative improvements – flexible housing that accommodates units other than nuclear families, appropriate accommodation for women who, for whatever reason, are leaving the matrimonial home (for example, battered women), accessible housing for the disabled and women with pushchairs and prams. Unemployment means something different when you are the first to lose your job, simply because you are female, and you know that there is always plenty of unpaid work waiting for you at home! More money and higher wages is a meaningless phrase when you have no personal disposable income to start off with, just 'the housekeeping'. When we oppose cuts in the services offered by the departments we work in, our emphasis must be not only on the retention of a service, but also on how it can be improved, democratized, and made responsive to real needs. We certainly do not just want more of the same. When we take political action in furtherance of our demands we must use our imagination to find forms of struggle that do not automatically alienate women or increase their hardship. In the past, trade union industrial action has done the latter on numerous occasions – the school caretakers' strike, for example, caused some working mothers to lose their jobs.

Sometimes alliances can be forged with sympathetic men. Several women in the group have joined the National Association of Probation Officers Members Action Group (NAMAG) and have found a forum for raising women's issues. However, there is a danger of becoming absorbed into primarily socialist, rather than feminist, issues. The collective action by women in the Action Group and the support of the Women in Social Work Group have been important in maintaining a feminist stand.

To some extent unions have to be played at their own game. In the West Midlands a group of probation officers has successfully obtained a mandate to organize a Sex Discrimination Working Party. This organization of a working party with report backs and the like, fits into union structure and has support for typing and duplication facilities. It is being used to gather information on sex discrimination, attitudes to women, and to bring the issues to people's attention. Without the support of the union such a project may have been disregarded in the agency. Unions will face women's issues put before them. For example, our local branch of the National Union of Public Employees (NUPE) made a financial gift to the Women's Aid squat in Birmingham, and did give our group some money when we started. The unions are a source of financial help, and, with no strings attached, should be used to the full. The National Association of Local Government Officers (NALGO) now has a full-time official dealing with sexual harassment at work, and her skills and time should be fully supported and used by women who need to understand the issues involved.

The frustrations and problems of working alongside men within our agencies are mirrored when we become involved with outside agencies and services that affect the lives of women. The police and social security are obvious examples, as are the medical and psychiatric services. The major force for change within these agencies must come from women working in them, but we can form alliances with some of these women through the Women's Liberation Movement. In our work we can support women in tackling the sexist attitudes by talking through issues, and helping them to compare notes and form alliances with other women. One woman in the group was able to support a woman client who was experiencing a destructive and distressing relationship with her GP, while trying to resolve various gynaecological and contraception problems. It was necessary to confront the GP directly with the consequence of his attitude but this was a difficult and painful experience for both women. In sharing this battle both emerged with a deeper understanding of each other's position.

Obviously our work involves direct contact with men and adolescent boys. Although, as we described earlier, when we are working with families, the woman in her caring and nurturing role often acts as the point of contact between the family and the Welfare State, even if the man is the client. Any consideration of how we can work with male clients and the effect on women of men in their lives is a mammoth task, and one beset with many difficulties. The relationship between a female worker and male client can in many ways replicate the male/female relationships in society. The client often has the expectations that the woman social worker will act in the role of wife, girlfriend, or mother.

In certain settings we find ourselves working with young single men, all of whom are oppressed in some way, because of class or race. We can help male clients improve their bargaining position in society. However, a dilemma we face daily is the feeling that we are unlikely to make much progress in influencing the sexist attitudes of our male clients because of other influences on them. They have an investment in maintaining the status quo, and yet we feel that we must find indirect ways of influencing them.

The main conclusion that we can draw from our discussions as a group is that raising the consciousness of male clients, in relation to masculinity and the way they relate to women, should be done by male colleagues. However, as we have discussed, changing the attitudes of male colleagues is an uphill struggle, and even if we have sympathetic male colleagues, men are not used to talking to each other on a personal level. As yet, men have not developed a language to discuss the personal and threatening aspects of male behaviour. We ask in fact whether we can, or must, trust our male colleagues to raise the issues we consider so crucial in a way we can support. We should not have to devote our time and energy to changing men's attitudes and behaviour. We must, of course, respond to women's requests for us to talk to their male partners (a refusal to talk with a violent partner may only reinforce the idea that men are unchallengeable). Working in situations involving a violent man poses further dilemmas. We reject the paternalistic notion that women need protecting. However, should we be placing ourselves at risk of physical injury? It is important that both male and female are able to look at their vulnerability when working with aggressive clients.

The ways in which our lives and our women clients' lives are constrained by men are our shared experiences. At this stage in the group we feel that how we deal with sexism and the effects of male behaviour on us is important, but we are only just beginning to work through these issues collectively with our sisters, colleagues, and clients.

When the group started, most of the women were on social work training courses. The group was very important to us all when we went back to various types and teams in social services and probation. We all understand now that what we have in common as feminists is far greater than the structural divisions of our work. Another development has been the group's relationship to the Women's Liberation Movement. When we started off some of us were unclear about the nature of our commitment to feminism, at that stage being more attracted by 'social work' in the name of the group. This has changed radically, both the group as a whole and individual women having developed a much firmer commitment to the Women's Movement.

One period of the group's history was most significant in the development of this commitment – the period surrounding the Feminism and Social Work Practice conference held at Warwick University in 1979. The organizers proposed and held a conference that was open to women and men. Our group argued, after discussion with the conference organizers, that the conference should be placed firmly within the politics of the Women's Movement and should not be open to men. The group felt it necessary to walk out of the plenary session in protest, as did other women present. Many of the women in the group before the conference were unfamiliar with the arguments and indeed all of us were daunted by the seeming radicalness and isolation of our stand.

But we emerged from this experience committed to the importance of allying ourselves to other women who are organizing around specific issues, for example: abortion, child care, and violence against women. Many of us have joined groups, like 'Women against the Cuts Group', as a direct result of our discussions about welfare provision and our position as state workers.

As well as raising common issues, the group plays a crucial role in providing support. By discussing problems we face at work (often it would seem those problems arising from our male colleagues and managers) we have developed the confidence to go back and stand up for what we want. For example, one woman who moved to residential work from fieldwork gained support by discussing with the group the new issues and difficulties she faced. Another example, which we have already discussed in this chapter, is the difficulties faced by women becoming active in their unions.

These functions of the group have, we hope, also been reflected in the national conferences and the open meetings we have organized locally. We have organized several series of open meetings. Other women from the Women's Liberation Movement have contributed on issues such as women and health, women and the law, and women and race. These meetings have increased our awareness and our membership. We remain committed to wanting other women to become involved and we have found it very important to be sensitive to the difficulties they may have in joining discussions. For example, we hold open meetings in public venues, rather than each other's homes. We feel that in doing so we make it less daunting for women to come to meetings. Holding open meetings also means that women who would not identify themselves as feminists have access to discussion of particular issues of interest to them. We have found that such women did come to specific meetings on this basis.

Reading this chapter, both our strengths and weaknesses as a group become apparent. We have attempted to place our personal experiences, particularly at work, in a specifically feminist political context. The nature of these experiences is therefore reflected in what we have included in our contribution to this book, as well as in the omissions. We would like to conclude this section by attempting to recognize these strengths and weaknesses and relating them to the history of the group and of the individual women involved.

First, we are conscious that we have not covered some very important areas within this chapter. In particular, we have not examined the position of black women, within a racist society, or the issues facing lesbians, as workers and clients. Our focus has also tended to be on the young (Phillipson 1981). In part, these omissions are a reflection of the composition of the group. They are also connected with the difficulties of discussing very personal issues within an open group whose primary aims have not been consciousness raising. All we can say is that we are aware of our omissions and we are trying to face the issues involved and expand our discussion.

In recognizing these gaps we have been made to realize how important writing this chapter has been for our group. We have had to think through our experiences and our politics in a more consistent way than before. This has given us all confidence and we can only urge other women to take such opportunities or to create them. From a position of strength we will start to influence women who have not had direct experience of the Women's Movement.

Afterword

EVE BROOK AND ANN DAVIS

This consideration of women, the family, and social work has focused in the main on work with and by women in the public services. It has not considered at length the work taking place in the voluntary and private spheres of welfare in Britain, some of which owes much to the influence of feminist thought and campaigning over the last decade or so. Our focus reflects the fact that all of our contributors have been involved in social work as practitioners, teachers (or both) in the public services and have written from that experience.

As employees in health, education, probation, and local authority services we share a number of common problems with millions of other public-sector women workers. Our experiences are also unique, for as professionally qualified women we are a minority group, with much larger salaries, greater job security and opportunities than other women employees. However, most state employment for women is not *just* a career, but one that is congruent with the things that women tend to give priority to – caring for people. As has been pointed out, women's socialization into femininity, primarily for the purpose of motherhood, makes them uniquely fitted for jobs involving the assessment and meeting of need (Norman and Mancuso 1980; Wilson 1980).

Indeed, Oakley (1979) sees the qualifications for motherhood as exactly the same as those required for the caring professions. She argues that a society that values tenderness, caring, and self-sacrifice in one sex has a very great need of the mother–child tie. What we have suggested in this book is that these connections must be more openly acknowledged and debated within social work training and practice. What is more, the problems of being a carer at home or in hierarchical welfare organizations need to be viewed from a perspective that recognizes that it is *women* who experience the problems most acutely.

Feminist thinking and the practice that has emerged from such projects as Women's Aid, Rape Crisis, and Women's Therapy has raised questions about the way in which state welfare agencies define and respond to social problems. The part that these agencies play in the creation as well as the alleviation of personal and social problems has been a matter for particular concern. For it not only affects the lives of women who become clients, but also the limits within which women as welfare workers can operate.

In a Britain with widespread unemployment and public-expenditure 'restraint' in state welfare, these questions take on a new urgency. The cuts in Welfare State expenditure, initiated in the 1970s and stepped up since 1979, mark a new era in welfare provision in Britain: an explicit attempt to restructure the Welfare State (Gough 1982; Glennerster 1980). This attempt has been characterized by an economic and ideological attack on the collective social provision of welfare services. Part of the ideological dimension of this attack has been to exhort the family to meet the needs of its members, rather than seek state help. This has, of course, major implications for women as workers in, and consumers of, Welfare State services.

As Edgell and Duke have shown (Edgell and Duke 1983:364) the predominance of women workers (most of whom are part time) in the education, health, and personal social services, has made women particularly vulnerable to the drop in employment levels in these services. In addition, the contraction of state services, such as care for pre-school children, has had direct effects on the employment opportunities for women who carry the main responsibility for child care within the home.

Central government and local authority policies that look to the increased use of 'community care' and 'informal networks' to replace residential and day care provision, are policies that are encouraging women to forget about paid employment outside the home and their desires to develop new interests (NISW 1982). They are also policies that refuse to face the fact that for those needing care and attention, alternatives to the family can offer positive experiences. A chance to establish a new way of life, new relationships, and a release from overburdening personal stresses and tensions.

To grasp some of the consequences of public expenditure cuts and government policies for women and their families, social workers must begin to look closely at how consumers experience the services they are offered and how they cope when services are no longer available. This requires a shift away from a concern with structures and quantity of provision, to a serious look at the quality of these provisions. Obviously, quality cannot be divorced from a consideration of resources but too often in the past quality has been defined and measured on professional criteria alone. Such criteria have reflected the concerns of professionals and administrators to safeguard their own work conditions and career opportunities, rather than an informed understanding of the choices open to clients. It should not, therefore, be surprising that consumers have proved reluctant to support campaigns to save services that they dread having to encounter, and find oppressive when they do. The suspicion on the consumers' part is that welfare workers, in trying to save services, are primarily interested in saving their jobs.

In campaigning within their agencies and beyond, social workers have been using a mixture of exposure politics and trade union activity. Very little thought has been given to examining parts of the provision that are welcomed by the consumer, and even less thought has gone into examining our own practices when we are actually delivering services to clients. One of the reasons for this is that such activities are seen as political and therefore separate from everyday practice. Those involved in politics as an 'after hours' activity may very well be reproducing during working hours relationships with clients that are oppressive and patriarchical. The contribution of feminism here, through the work of women and social work groups, is to show that politics can be an important element in everyday work. It is a continuing part of examining both personal practice and the woman's role in her agency, and can lead to creative work with clients.

The reason for this is that feminism does not make the split between politics and the way in which one behaves towards other people, especially other people over whom one has power. Feminism places great emphasis on everyday conduct and activity that means living as a feminist *now*, not later, or after working hours. It suggests that clients have to be brought into the debate about women and welfare in new ways – ways that are at odds with the notion of waiting until after 'the social work intervention' to assess 'worker effectiveness' by measuring client 'change'.

Britain in the 1980s is going to throw into sharp relief the question of women, the family, and social work. For in a period of economic recession inequalities between men and women are likely to increase. The contribution that feminism has to make to understanding and working with the inequalities and contradictions produced is substantial, as it refuses to ignore the links between the personal and political, the public and the private.

References

Abbott, E. and Bompass, K. (1943) *The Woman Citizen and Social Security: A Criticism of the Proposals in the Beveridge Report as they Affect Women*. Women's Freedom League Pamphlet.

Abrams, M. (1980) *Beyond Three-Score Years and Ten*. London: Age Concern.

Ackerman, N. S. (1958) *Psychodynamics of Family Life*. New York: Basic Books.

Age Concern (1981) *Profiles of the Elderly: Their Use of Social Services* **8**. London: Age Concern.

Allen, M. and Nicholson, M. (1967) *Memoirs of an Uneducated Lady – Lady Allen of Hurtwood*. London: Thames & Hudson.

Allen, S., Sanders, L., and Wallis, J. (eds) (1974) *Conditions of Illusion*. Leeds: Feminist Books.

Arie, T. (1977) Psychiatric care of the elderly. In A. N. Exton-Smith and J. G. Evans (eds) *Care of the Elderly: Meeting the Challenge of Dependency*. London: Academic Press.

Armitage, M. (1979) The cost of caring for the elderly. *Social Work Today* **10** (38): 15–16.

Ashworth, R. (1979) Fair do's for women in local government. *Local Government Review* 27 January.

Association of Community Workers (1982) *Women and Collective Action*. ACW.

Aves, G. M. (1969) *The Voluntary Worker in the Social Services*. London: Allen & Unwin.

Badninter, E. (1981) *The Myth of Motherhood*. London: Souvenir Press.

Bailey, R. and Brake, M. (1980) *Radical Social Work and Practice*. London: Edward Arnold.

Bailey, R. and Lee, P. (1982) *Theory and Practice in Social Work*. Oxford: Basil Blackwell.

Baker Miller, J. (1978) *Towards a New Psychology of Women*. Harmondsworth: Penguin.

Barker, D. and Allen, S. (eds) (1976) *Sexual Divisions and Society: Process and Change*. London: Tavistock Publications.

Barker, J. (1980) The relationship of 'informal' care to 'formal' social services: who helps people deal with social and health problems if they arise in old age? In S. Lonsdale, A. Webb, and T. L. Briggs (eds) *Teamwork in the Personal Social Services and Health Care: British and American Perspectives*. London: Croom Helm.

Barrett, M. (1980) *Women's Oppression Today: Problems in Marxist Feminist Analysis*. London: New Left Books.

Barrett, M. and McIntosh, M. (1983) *The Anti Social Family*. London: Verso.

Barron, R. D. and Norris, G. M. (1976) Sexual divisions in the dual labour market. In B. L. Barker and S. Allen, (eds) *Dependence and Exploitation in Work and Marriage*. London: Longman.

Bebbington, A. (1979) Changes in the provision of social services to the elderly in the community over 14 years. *Journal of Social Policy and Administration* **13** (2).

Bem, S. L. (1974) The measurement of psychological androgyny. *Journal of Consulting and Clinical Psychology* **42**: 155–62.

Bland, L., Brunsdon, C., Hobson, D., and Winship, D. (1978) Women inside and outside the relations of production. In the Centre for Contemporary Cultural Studies, Birmingham, *Women Take Issue*. London: Hutchinson.

Block, J., Von Der Lippe, A., and Block, J. H. (1973) Sex role and socialisation patterns: some personality concomitants and environmental antecedents. *Journal of Consulting and Clinical Psychology* **41**: 321–41.

Bone, M. (1977) *Pre-school Children and Their Need for Day Care*. London: HMSO.

Bottomore, T. (1962) *Sociology: a guide to problems and literature*. London: Allen & Unwin.

Bowlby, J. (1953) *Child Care and the Growth of Love*. London: Pelican.

Brearley, C. P. (1974) *Self-help, Participation and the Elderly*. Southampton University.

—— (1975) *Social Work, Ageing and Society*. London: Routledge & Kegan Paul.

—— (1977) *Residential Work with the Elderly*. London: Routledge & Kegan Paul.

—— (1978) Ageing and social work. In D. Hobman (ed.) *The Social Challenge of Ageing*. London: Croom Helm.

British Association of Social Workers (1977) Guidelines for social work with the elderly. *Social Work Today* **8** (27):7–15.

—— (1982) *Services for Elderly People*. Birmingham: BASW.

Brook, D. (1976) *Nature Birth*. Harmondsworth: Penguin.

Broverman, I. K., Broverman, D. M., Clarkson, F. E., Rosenkrantz, P. R., and Vogt, S. R. (1970) Sex role stereotypes and clinical judgements of mental health. *Journal of Consulting and Clinical Psychology* **34**:1–7.

Brown, G. W., Ni Bhrolchain, M., and Harris, T. O. (1975) Social class and psychiatric disturbance among women in an urban population. *Sociology* **9**:225–54.

Brown, G. W. and Harris, T. (1978) *Social Origins of Depression*. London: Tavistock.

Butler, P. (1976) Assertive training and teaching women not to discriminate against themselves. *Psychotherapy Theory, Research and Practice* **13**:55–60.

Calder, A. (1969) *The People's War*. London: Panther.

Cardiff University Social Services (1976) CUSS Group Homes.

Central Statistical Office (1981) *Economic Trends*. December. London: HMSO.

Chalmers, I. and Richards, M. (1977) Intervention and causal inference. In T. Chard and M. Richards (eds) *Benefits and Hazards of the New Obstetrics*. London: Heinemann.

Chernin, K. (1983) *Womansize: the Tyranny of Slenderness*. London: The Women's Press.

Chesler, P. (1971) Women as psychiatric and psychotherapeutic patients. *Journal of Marriage and the Family* **33**:746–59.

—— (1974) *Women and Madness*. London: Allen Lane.

Chodorow, N. (1978) *The Reproduction of Mothering*. Berkeley, CA: University of California Press.

Christian Economic and Social Research Foundation (1957) *Youth Mothers at Work*. London.

Clancy, K. and Gove, W. R. (1974) Sex differences in mental illness: an analysis of response bias in self-reports. *American Journal of Psychotherapy* **80**:205–16.

Clare, A. (1980) *Psychiatry in Dissent*. London: Tavistock Publications.

Clarke, J., Langan, M., and Lee, P. (1982) Social work: the conditions of crisis. In P. Carlen and M. Collison (eds) *Radical Issues in Criminology*. Oxford: Martin Robertson.

Connolly, J. (1847) The Construction and Government of Lunatic Asylums, *Psychiatric Monograph* **6**. London: Dawsons, 1968.

Cooper, J. D. (1980) *Social Group Work with Elderly People in Hospital*. University of Keele: Beth Johnson Foundation.

Cooper, M. A., Mooring, J. L., and Scott, J. A. (1975) *Neighbourhood Work*. Wakefield Social Services Department.

Coote, A. and Campbell, B. (1982) *Sweet Freedom*. London: Picador.

Corrigan, P. and Leonard, P. (1978) *Social Work Practice Under Capitalism: A Marxist Approach*. London: Macmillan.

Coward, R. (1979) Significant thinker. *New Forum* **5**:51–3.

Darville, G. (1975) *Bargain or Barricade?* Volunteer Centre, Berkhamsted.

Davis, A. (1980) Personally speaking. *Community Care* 10 July.

—— (1981) *The Residential Solution*. London: Tavistock Publications.

Deacon, A. and Hill, M. (1972) The Problem of 'Surplus Women' in the Nineteenth Century: Secular and Religious Alternatives. *A Sociological Yearbook of Religion in Britain* **V**. London: SCM Press.

Delphy, C. (1980) A materialist feminism is possible. *Feminist Review* **4**.

DHSS (1975) *Better Services for the Mentally Ill*. London: HMSO.

—— (1977) *Inpatient Statistics for the Mental Health Enquiry for England 1975*, Statistics and Research Report Series 20. London: HMSO.

Dinnerstein, D. (1978) *The Rocking of the Cradle*. London: Souvenir Press.

Dohrenwend, B. P. (1975) Sociocultural and social-psychological factors in the genesis of mental disorders. *Journal of Health and Social Behaviour* **16**:365–92.

Dominelli, L. and McLeod, E. (1982) The personal and the a-political: feminism and moving beyond the Integrated Methods

Approach. In R. Bailey and P. Lee, *Theory and Practice in Social Work*. Oxford: Basil Blackwell.

Edgell, S. and Duke, V. (1983) Gender and social policy: the impact of the public expenditure cuts and reactions to them. *Journal of Social Policy* **12**(3):357–78.

Ehrenreich, B. and English, D. (1979) *For Her Own Good*. London: Pluto Press.

Eichenbaum, L. and Orbach, S. (1982) *Outside In, Inside Out*. Harmondsworth: Penguin.

—— (1983) *What do Women Want?* London: Michael Joseph.

Einstein, A. (1934) *The World As I See It*. London: Bodley Head.

Elliott, D. (1978) Integrated Methods and Residential Work. *Social Work Today* **9**(24).

Equal Opportunities Commission (1979) EOC Response to the DHSS Discussion Document 'A Happier Old Age'. London: EOC.

—— (1980) *The Experience of Caring for Elderly and Handicapped Dependants*. A Survey Report. Manchester: EOC.

—— (1981) *Behind Closed Doors*. Manchester: EOC.

—— (1982) *Women in Public Life*. Manchester: EOC.

Evers, H. (1981) Care or custody? The experiences of women patients in long-stay geriatric wards. In B. Hutter and U. William (eds) *Controlling Women. The Normal and the Deviant*. London: Croom Helm.

Filkin, G. (1978) Special housing needs – Why so special? *Volunteer Housing*. September.

Finch, J. and Groves, D. (1980) Community care and the family: a case for equal opportunities? *Journal of Social Policy* **9**(4): 487–511.

—— (1981) By women, for women: caring for the frail elderly. *Women's Studies International Quarterly* **5**(5).

—— (eds) (1983) *A Labour of Love: Women, Work and Caring*. London: Routledge & Kegan Paul.

Fitzgerald, T. (1983) The New Right and the family. In M. Loney, D. Boswell, and J. Clarke, (eds) *Social Policy and Social Welfare*. Milton Keynes: The Open University.

Fogarty, M., Rapoport, R., and Rapoport, R. (1971) *Sex, Career and Family*. London: Allen & Unwin.

Fraser, R. (ed.) (1969) *Work 2*. Harmondsworth: Penguin.

Friedman, H. J. (1975) Special problems of women in psychotherapy. *American Journal of Psychotherapy* **20**:405–16.

Gavron, H. (1966) *The Captive Wife.* London: Routledge & Kegan Paul.

Ginsburg, N. (1979) *Class, Capital and Social Policy.* London: Macmillan Press.

Glennerster, H. (1980) Public spending and the social services: the end of an era? In M. Brown and S. Baldwin (eds) *Yearbook of Social Policy in Britain, 1979.* London: Routledge & Kegan Paul.

Goffman, E. (1961) *Asylums. Essays on the Social Situation of Mental Patients and Other Inmates.* Harmondsworth: Penguin.

Goldberg, E. M. (1979) *Social Work since Seebohm: All Things to All Men.* London: National Institute for Social Work.

Goldberg, E. M., Mortimer, A., and Williams, B. T. (1970) *Helping the Aged: A Field Experiment in Social Work.* London: Allen & Unwin.

Goldberg, E. M. and Warburton, R. W. (1979) *Ends and Means in Social Work.* London: Allen & Unwin.

Goldberg, E. M., Warburton, R. W., McGuiness, B., and Rowlands, J. M. (1977) Towards accountability in social work: one year's intake to an area office. *British Journal of Social Work* 7(3):255–83.

Goldberg, E. M., Warburton, R. W., Lyons, L. J., and Willmott, R. R. (1978) Towards accountability in social work: long term social work in an area office. *British Journal of Social Work* 8(3): 253–87.

Goldstein, H. (1973) *Social Practice: A Unitary Approach.* Columbia, SC: University of South Carolina Press.

—— (1977) Theory development and the unitary approach to social work practice. In H. Specht and A. Vickery (eds) *Integrating Social Work Methods.* London: Allen & Unwin.

Gore, S. and Mangoine, T. W. (1983) Social Roles, Sex Roles and Psychological Distress: Additive and Interactive Models of Sex Differences. *Journal of Health and Social Behaviour* 24:300–01.

Gough, I. (1982) The crisis of the British Welfare State. In N. Fainstein and S. Fainstein (eds) *Urban Policy Under Capitalism.* London: Sage Publications.

Gouldner, A. (1971) *The Coming Crisis of Western Sociology.* London: Heinemann.

Gove, W. R. (1978) Sex differences in mental illness among adult men and women. *Social Science and Medicine* 12(3):187–98.

Government Actuary (1981) *Occupational Pensions Schemes 1979.* Sixth Survey. London: HMSO.

Grafton, P. (1982) *You, You and You: The People Out of Step with World War Two*. London: Pluto Press.

Graham, H. (1977) Images of pregnancy in ante-natal literature. In R. Dingwall, C. Heath, M. Reid, and M. Stacey (eds) *Health Care and Health Knowledge*. London: Croom Helm.

Gregory, J. (1979) Equal pay and sex discrimination: why women are giving up the fight. *Feminist Review* **10**.

Groves, D. (1983) Members and survivors: women and retirement pensions legislation. In J. Lewis (ed.) *Women's Welfare: Women's Rights*. London: Croom Helm.

—— (forthcoming) *Women and Occupational Pensions: An Exploratory Study*. (Ph.D. thesis to be submitted to the University of London.)

Groves, D. and Finch, J. (1983) Natural selection: perspectives on entitlement to the invalid care allowance. In J. Finch and D. Groves (eds) *A Labour of Love: Women, Work and Caring*. London: Routledge & Kegan Paul.

Hadley, R. (1981) Social services departments and the community. In E. M. Goldberg and S. Hatch (eds) *A New Look at the Personal Social Services*. PSI Discussion Paper **4**. London: Policy Studies Institute.

Hadley, R. and McGrath, M. (1980) *Going Local*. NCVO Occasional Paper **1**. London: National Council for Voluntary Organisations.

Hale, J. (1983) Feminism and social work practice. In B. Jordan and N. Parton *The Political Dimensions of Social Work*. Oxford: Basil Blackwell.

Hall, C. (1982a) The home turned upside down? The working-class family in cotton textiles 1780–1850. In E. Whitelegg, M. Arnott, E. Bartels, V. Beelhey, L. Buke, S. Himmelweit, D. Leonard, S. Ruehl, and M. Speakman, (eds) *The Changing Experience of Women*. Oxford: Martin Robertson.

—— (1982b) The butcher, the baker, the candlestick maker: the shop and the family in the Industrial Revolution. In E. Whitelegg, M. Arnot, E. Bartels, V. Beelhey, L. Buke, S. Himmelweit, D. Leonard, S. Ruehl, and M. Speakman (eds) *The Changing Experience of Women*. Oxford: Martin Robertson.

Hall, J. E. and Hare-Mustin, R. (1983) Sanctions and the diversity of ethical complaints against psychologists. *American Psychologist* **38**:714–29.

Hall, T. and Hall, P. (eds) (1980) *Part-time Social Work*. London: Heinemann.

Handler, J. (1968) The coercive child care officer. *New Society* **12**:314.

Hare, E. H. and Shaw, G. K. (1965) *Mental Health on a New Housing Estate*. London: Oxford University Press.

Haringey and Lewisham Women's Employment Project (1981) *Women Where are your Jobs Going?*

Hartmann, H. (1979) The unhappy marriage of marxism and feminism: towards a more progressive union. *Capital and Class* **8**:1–33.

Health Advisory Service Annual Report (1976): 331–32.

HMSO (1946) *Report of the Care of Children Committee* (The Curtis Report). Cmnd. 6922, London: HMSO.

—— (1960) *The Report of the Committee on Children and Young Persons* (Ingleby). Cmnd. 1191, London: HMSO.

—— (1967) *The Place of Voluntary Service in After-Care*. Second Report of Working Party (Reading), London: HMSO.

—— (1974) *Women and Work: A Statistical Survey*. Manpower Paper **9** Department of Employment.

—— (1974) *Report of the Committee on One Parent Families* (Finer) **I** and **II**. Cmnd. 5269, London: HMSO.

—— (1976) *DHSS Personal Social Services Local Authority Statistics*. London: HMSO.

—— (1976) *Report of the Working Party on Manpower and Training for the Social Services* (Birch). London: HMSO.

—— (1982) *Social Trends 1983*. London: HMSO.

Hewitt, M. (1958) *Wives and Mothers in Victorian Industry*. London: Barrie & Rockcliff.

Hollis, P. (1979) *Women in Public: The Women's Movement 1850–1900*. London: Allen & Unwin.

Holloway, E. (1980) Social work with elderly disabled people – *not* 'downhill all the way'. *Social Work Service* **24**:14–17.

Holman, R. (1976) *Child Care and Inequality*. Child Poverty Action Group.

Holme, A. and Maizels, J. (1978) *Social Work and Volunteers*. London: BASW and Allen & Unwin.

Holroyd, J. C. and Brodsky, A. M. (1977) Psychologists' attitudes and practices regarding erotic and nonerotic physical contact with patients. *American Psychologist* **32**:843–49.

Hope, E., Kennedy, M., and De Winter, A. (1976) Homeworkers in

North London. In S. L. Barker and S. Allen (eds) *Dependence and Exploitation in Work and Marriage*. London: Longman.

Horner, M. S. (1972) Towards an understanding of achievement-related conflict in women. *Journal of Social Issues* **28**:157–75.

Hubback, J. (1957) *Wives who Went to College*. London: Heinemann.

Hugman, R. (1981) Images of the elderly: a different slant on fostering. *Community Care* **425**:12–13.

Hunt, A. (1968) *A Survey of Women's Employment*. London: HMSO.

—— (1975) *Management Attitudes and Practices Towards Women at Work*. London: HMSO.

—— (1978) *The Elderly at Home*. Office of Population Census and Surveys. London: HMSO.

Hutter, B. and Williams, G. (eds) (1981) *Controlling Women: The Normal and the Deviant*. London: Croom Helm.

Jefferys, M. (1977) The elderly in the United Kingdom. In A. N. Exton-Smith and J. G. Evans (eds) *Caring for the Elderly: Meeting the Challenge of Dependency*. London: Academic Press.

Jephcott, P., Seear, N., and Smith, J. H. (1962) *Married Women Working*. London: Allen & Unwin.

Jones, C. (1979) Social Work Education 1900–77. In N. Parry, M. Rustin, and C. Satyamurti (eds) *Social Work and the State*. London: Edward Arnold.

Jones, H. (ed.) (1975) *Towards a New Social Work*. London: Routledge & Kegan Paul.

Jordan, B. (1974) *Poor Parents: Social Policy and the Cycle of Deprivation*. London: Routledge & Kegan Paul.

—— (1977) Against the Unitary approach to social work. *New Society* 2 June.

Jordan, B. and Parton, N. (1983) *The Political Dimensions of Social Work*. Oxford: Basil Blackwell.

Kahn, M. M. R. (1975) Grudge and hysteric. *International Journal of Psychoanalytic Psychotherapy* **4**:349–57.

Kaplan, M. (1983) A woman's view of DSM III. *American Psychologist* **38**:786–92.

Kent Community Care Project (1979) *An Interim Report: Personal Social Services Research Unit*. Canterbury: University of Kent.

Kirsh, B. (1974) Consciousness-raising groups as therapy for women. In V. Franks and V. Burtle (eds) *Women in Therapy*. New York: Brunner/Mazel.

Land, H. (1976) Women: Supporters or Supported? In D. L. Barker and S. Allen (eds) *Sexual Divisions and Society*. London: Tavistock Publications.

—— (1978) Who cares for the family? *Journal of Social Policy* **7**(3):357–84.

—— (1979) The boundaries between the state and the family. In C. Harris (ed.) *The Sociology of the Family: New Directions for Britain*. Sociological Review Monograph **28**. University of Keele.

Lawrence, M. (1984) *The Anorexic Experience*. London: The Women's Press.

Lees, R. and Smith, G. (1975) *Action-Research in Community Development*. London: Routledge & Kegan Paul.

Leeson, J. and Gray, J. (1978) *Women and Medicine*. London: Tavistock Publications.

Leonard, P. (1975) Towards a paradigm for radical practice. In R. Bailey and M. Brake (eds) *Radical Social Work*. London: Edward Arnold.

Levy, P. (1981) On the relation between method and substance in psychology. *Bulletin of the British Psychological Society* **34**:265–70.

Lewis, J. (1980) *The Politics of Motherhood*. London: Croom Helm.

—— (ed.) (1983) *Women's Welfare: Women's Rights*. London: Croom Helm.

Litman, G. K. (1977) Clinical aspects of sex-role stereotyping. In J. Chetwynd and O. Hartnett (eds) *The Sex-role System*. London: Routledge & Kegan Paul.

Llewelyn, S. and Kelly, J. (1979) Values, politics and individualism in psychology: a case for a new paradigm? *Bulletin of the British Psychological Society* **33**:407–11.

Llewelyn, S. and Osborne, K. (1983) Women as clients. In D. Pilgrim (ed.) *Psychology and Psychotherapy, Current Trends and Issues*. London: Routledge & Kegan Paul.

Lomax, M. (1921) *The Experiences of an Asylum Doctor*. London: Allen & Unwin.

Lyttleton, Hon. Mrs A. (1901) *The Ladies Year Book*. London: Adam & Charles Black.

MacIntyre, S. (1976) Who wants babies? The social construction of instincts. In D. Barker and S. Allen (eds) *Sexual Divisions and Society: Process and Change*. London: Tavistock Publications.

Macleod, S. (1981) *The Art of Starvation*. London: Virago.

Macoby, E. E. and Jacklin, C. N. (1975) *The Psychology of Sex Differences*. London: Oxford University Press.

Marris, P. (1958) *Widows and Their Families*. London: Routledge & Kegan Paul.

Mayo, M. (1977) *Women in the Community*. London: Routledge & Kegan Paul.

Mead, M. (1935) *Sex and Temperament in Three Primitive Societies*. New York: William Morrow.

Miles, J. (1981) Sexism in social work. *Social Work Today* **13**(1).

MIND/Community Care (1976) Ready to leave? A survey on rehabilitation and after care for mentally ill patients. *Community Care* 23 June: 16–24.

MIND (1982) Evidence to the Royal Commission on the National Health Service. London: MIND.

Mishra, R. (1983) *The Welfare State in Crisis*. Brighton: Wheatsheaf Books

Mitchell, J. (1971) *Woman's Estate*. Harmondsworth: Penguin.

—— (1974) *Psychoanalysis and Feminism*. London: Allen Lane.

Myrdal, A. and Klein, V. (1956) *Women's Two Roles*. London: Routledge & Kegan Paul.

Nairne, K. and Smith, G. (1984) *Dealing with Depression*. London: The Women's Press.

National Institute for Social Work (1982) *Social Workers: Their Role and Tasks* (The Barclay Report). London: Bedford Square Press.

Newton, N. and Newton, M. (1972) Childbirth. In J. G. Howells (ed.) *Modern Perspectives in Psycho-obstetrics* London: Oliver & Boyd.

Norman, E. and Mancuso, A. (1980) *Women's Issues and Social Work Practice*. Itasca, IL: F. E. Peacock.

Oakley, A. (1972) *Sex, Gender and Society*. London: Maurice Temple Smith.

—— (1974) *Housewife*. London: Allen Lane.

—— (1979) *From Here to Maternity: Becoming a Mother*. Harmondsworth: Pelican.

—— (1980) *Women Confined*. Oxford: Martin Robertson.

—— (1981) *Subject Women*. New York: Pantheon Books.

Oakley, A. and Oakley, R. (1979) Sexism in official statistics. In J. Irvine, I. Miles and J. Evans (eds) *Demystifying Social Statistics*. London: Pluto Press.

Office of Population, Censuses and Surveys (1978) *Demographic Review 1977*. Series DR, **1**. London: HMSO.

—— (1979) *General Household Survey 1978*. Social Survey Division, Series GMS, **8**. London: HMSO.

—— (1980) *Marriage and Divorce Statistics 1978*. Series FM2, **5**. London: HMSO.

Orbach, S. (1978) *Fat is a Feminist Issue*. Feltham: Hamlyn.

Parker, R. (1981) Tending and social policy. In E. M. Goldberg and S. Hatch (eds) *A New Look at the Personal Social Services*. PSI Discussion Paper No. 4. London: Policy Studies Institute.

Parry, N. and Parry, J. (1979) *Social Work, Professionalism and the State*. London: Edward Arnold.

Parsloe, P. (1972) Cross sex supervision in the probation and after-care service. *British Journal of Criminology*. **12**(3).

Parsons, T. (1951) *The Social System*. London: Routledge & Kegan Paul.

Phillipson, C. (1981) Women in later life: patterns of control and subordination. In B. Hutter and G. Williams (eds) *Controlling Women: The Normal and the Deviant*. London: Croom Helm.

Piachaud, D. (1981) *Children and Poverty*. Child Poverty Action Group.

Pincus, A. and Minahan, A. (1973) *Social Work Practice Model and Method*. Itasca, IL: F. E. Peacock.

—— (1977) A model for social work practice. In H. Specht and A. Vickery (eds) *Integrating Social Work Methods*. London: Allen & Unwin.

Pincus, L. (ed.) (1953) *Social Casework in Marital Problems*. London: Tavistock Publications.

Pope, P. (1980) Emergency admissions into homes for the elderly. *Social Work Service* **24**:18–22.

Popplestone, R. (1980) Top jobs for women: are the cards stacked against them? *Social Work Today* **12**(4).

—— (1981) *A Women's Profession?* (Unpublished paper given at the Feminism and Social Work Conference, University of Bradford, 22 March.)

Poster, M. (1978) *Critical Theory of the Family*. London: Pluto Press.

Procter, H. G. and Parry, G. (1978) Constraint and freedom: the social origin of personal constructs. In F. Fransella (ed.) *Personal Construct Theory 1977*. London: Academic Press.

Rapaport, R. and Fogarty, M. P. (1982) *Families in Britain*. London: Routledge & Kegan Paul.

Reeves, M. P. (1979) *Round About a Pound a Week*. London: Virago.

Residential Child Care Association (1965) *Change and the Child in Care*. Proceedings of the Annual Review of the RCCA.

Rich, A. (1977) *Of Woman Born: Motherhood as Experience and Institution*. London: Virago.

Riley, D. (1983) *War in the Nursery – Theories of the Child and Mother*. London: Virago.

Rimmer, L. (1981) *Families in Focus: Marriage, Divorce and Family Pattern*. London: Study Commission on the Family.

Roberts, H. (ed.) (1981) *Women, Health and Reproduction*. London: Routledge & Kegan Paul.

Rodgers, B. (1963) *A Follow-Up Study of Social Administration Students, Manchester University (1940–60)*. Manchester: Manchester University Press.

Rowlings, C. (1981) *Social Work with Elderly People*. London: Allen & Unwin.

Salwen, L. H. (1975) New conflicts for the new woman. *Psychotherapy Theory, Research and Practice* **12**:429–52.

Sarason, I. G. and Smith, R. E. (1971) Personality. *Annual Review of Psychology* **22**:393–446.

Satyamurti, C. (1979) Care and control in local authority social work. In N. Parry, M. Rustin, and C. Satyamurti (eds) *Social Work and the State*. London: Edward Arnold.

Seebohm Report (1968) *Report of the Committee on Local Authority and Allied Personal Social Services*. Cmnd 3703. London: HMSO.

Segal, L. (ed.) (1983) *What is to be Done about the Family?* Harmondsworth: Penguin.

Seiden, A. (1976) Overview: research on the psychology of women. *American Journal of Psychiatry* **133**:995–1007, 1111–123.

Shapiro, M. B. (1979) The social origins of depression, in G. W. Brown and T. Harris; its methodological philosophy. *Behaviour, Research and Therapy* (forthcoming).

Shepherd, M., Cooper, B., Brown, A. C. and Kalton, G. W. (1966) *Psychiatric Illness in General Practice*. London: Oxford University Press.

Sherfey, M. J. (1972) *The Nature and Evolution of Female Sexuality*. New York: Random House.

Skeet, M. and Crout, E. (1977) *Health Needs Help*. London: Blackwell Scientific Publications.

Smart, C. and Smart, B. (eds) (1978) *Women, Sexuality and Social Control*. Routledge & Kegan Paul.

Socialist Medical Association (1964) *A Socialist View of Social Work*.

Specht, H. (1977) Social trends. In H. Specht and A. Vickery *Integrating Social Work Methods*. London: Allen & Unwin.

Spence, J. T. (1979) Traits, roles and the concept of adrogyny. In J. E. Gullahorn (ed) *Psychology and Women: in Transition*. Winston: Wiley.

Spence, J. T. and Helmreich, R. (1972) Who likes competent women? Competence, sex-role congruence of interests and subjects attitudes to women as determinants of interpersonal attraction. *Journal of Applied Social Psychology* **2**:197–213.

Spring Rice, M. (1939) *Working Class Wives*. London: Virago, 1981.

Statham, D. (1978) *Radicals in Social Work*. London: Routledge & Kegan Paul.

Steadman Jones, G. (1971) *Outcast London: A Study in the Relationship Between Classes in Victorian Society*. London: Oxford University Press.

Stearns, P. N. (1977) *Old Age in European Society*. London: Croom Helm.

Stein, Z. and Susser, M. (1969) Widowhood and mental illness. *British Journal of Preventive and Social Medicine* **232**:106.

Stevenson, O. and Parsloe, P. (1978) *Social Services Teams: The Practitioner's View*. London: HMSO.

Szasz, T. (1974) *Law, Liberty and Psychiatry*. London: Routledge & Kegan Paul.

Tennant, C. and Bebbington, P. (1979) The social causation of depression: a critique of the work of Brown and his colleagues. *Psychological Medicine* **8**:565–75.

Thane, P. (1978) The muddled history of retiring at 60 and 65. *New Society* **45**(826):234–36.

Timms, N. (1964) *Social Casework*. London: Routledge & Kegan Paul.

—— (1967) *Psychiatric Social Work in Great Britain*. London: Routledge & Kegan Paul.

Titmuss, R. (1950) *Problems of Social Policy*. London: HMSO and Longman.

—— (1958) *Essays on the Welfare State*. London: Allen & Unwin.

Townsend, P. and Abel-Smith, B. (1965) *The Poor and the Poorest*. London: Bell & Hyman.

Townsend, P. (1979) *Poverty in the United Kingdom*. Harmondsworth: Allen Lane and Penguin Books.

—— (1981) The structured dependency of the elderly: a creation of social policy in the twentieth century. *Ageing and Society* **1**(1):5–28.

Treacher, A. (1979) The politics of psychotherapy. *New Forum* **5**:63–4.

Trevelyan, J. (1954) *Two Stories*. London: Spottiswoode.

Tudor, W., Tudor, J. F. and Gove, W. R. (1977) The effect of sex role differences on the social control of mental illness. *Journal of Health and Social Behaviour* **18**:98–112.

United Nations Economic Commission for Europe (1977) *Housing for Special Groups*. Proceedings of an International Seminar on Housing for Special Groups. Oxford: Pergamon Press.

Vickery, A. (1977) Social casework. In H. Specht and A. Vickery (eds) *Integrating Social Work Methods*. London: Allen & Unwin.

Walker, A. (1981) Towards a political economy of old age. *Ageing and Society* **1**(1):73–94.

Walker, H. and Beaumont, B. (1981) *Probation Work: Critical Theory and Socialist Practice*. London: Basil Blackwell.

Waller, K. (1976) Social worker attitudes to women. Report to CCETSW unpublished, quoted in C. Jasilek, *Women and Welfare*. Media Booklet, Milton Keynes: The Open University, 1979.

Walrond Skinner, S. (1976) *Family Therapy, The Treatment of Natural Systems*. London: Routledge & Kegan Paul.

Walton, R. (1975) *Women and Social Work*. London: Routledge & Kegan Paul.

Warren, L. and McEachren, L. (1983) Psychosocial Correlates of Depressive Symptomatology in Adult Women. *Journal of Abnormal Psychology* **92**:157–60.

Webb, B. (1926) *Our Partnership*. London: Longmans.

Webb, L. J. and Allen, R. (1979) Sex differences in mental health. *Journal of Psychology* **101**:89–96.

Weir, A. (1974) The family, social work and the welfare state. In S. Allen, L. Sanders, and J. Wallis (eds) *Conditions of Illusion*. Leeds: Feminist Books.

Weissman, M. M. and Klerman, G. (1977) Sex differences and the epidemiology of depression. *Archives of General Psychiatry* **34**:98–101.

Whitelegg, E., Arnot, M., Bartels, E., Beelhey, V., Buke, L., Himmelweit, S., Leonard, D., Ruehl, S., and Speakman, M. (eds) (1982) *The Changing Experience of Women*. Oxford: Martin Robertson.

Wilkins, D. (1979) *Caring for the Mentally Handicapped Child*. London: Croom Helm.

The Williams Report (1967) *Caring for People: Staffing Residential Homes*. London: Allen & Unwin.

Wilson, E. (1977) *Women and the Welfare State*. London: Tavistock Publications.

—— (1979) Guilt-edged security. *New Forum* **5**:57–8.

—— (1980) *Only Half-way to Paradise: Women in Post War Britain 1945–1968*. London: Tavistock Publications.

—— (1983a) *What is to be Done about Violence towards Women?* Harmondsworth: Penguin.

—— (1983b) Feminism and Social Policy. In M. Loney, D. Boswell, and J. Clarke, *Social Policy and Social Welfare*. Milton Keynes: the Open University.

Womens Group on Public Welfare (1948) *The Neglected Child and His Family*. London: Oxford University Press.

Wootton, B. (1959) *Social Science and Social Pathology*. London: Routledge & Kegan Paul.

Worrall, A. (1981) Out of place: female offenders in court. *Probation Journal* **28**(3).

Young, M. (ed.) (1974) *Poverty Report*. London: Maurice Temple Smith.

—— (ed.) (1975) *Poverty Report*. London: Maurice Temple Smith.

Younghusband, E. (1947) *Report on the Employment and Training of Social Workers*. Carnegie UK Trust.

—— (1951) *Social Work in Britain*. Carnegie UK Trust.

Name index

Subject index